Defender of the Damned:
GLADYS TOWLES ROOT

OTHER BOOKS BY CY RICE

One for the Book (with Sam Balter)
Man with a Racket (with Pancho Gonzales)
My Eyes Are in My Heart (with Ted Husing)
Erroll and Me (with Nora Eddington Flynn Haymes)
Cleopatra in Mink

defender
of the
damned:

GLADYS TOWLES ROOT

by CY RICE

THE CITADEL PRESS   *New York*

For Blanche, Kathryn, and "Fritzie"

Contents

INTRODUCTION

From the mansions and estates of Bel Air, Brentwood, Beverly Hills, Trousdale, Santa Barbara, San Marino and Pasadena to the dingy dives of Los Angeles' Skid Row, they speak of Gladys Towles Root, criminal lawyer. Yet, how many who freely drop her name really know her?

After eight months of close working contact, I wonder if I really do.

Upon first meeting her, the bizarre dress, the way-out coiffure, the huge custom-made jewelry, the boundless energy, the sharp mind that needs no prodding to start in motion, are overwhelming. She reminded me of a Technicolor pinwheel in perpetual motion in Cinemascope.

Gladys Root is one of America's most successful criminal lawyers. She has won more sex cases than any lawyer in the United States. Her specialty is defending alleged homosexuals, child molesters, prostitutes, rapists, peeping Toms; she also handles murder accusations, paternity suits, divorces and bigamy cases.

A campaigner in a controversial field, she began accepting morals cases as a matter of principle when other attorneys refused. Her regal bearing, eccentric costumes, and sensational bag of legal tricks have packed the Los Angeles courtrooms.

The press has acclaimed the five-foot eleven-inch Junoesque blonde as the most spectacular showwoman to appear on the local scene since Aimee Semple McPherson.

To examine her objectively, to wade through the flash and dazzle of her exterior and penetrate to her brain, isn't easy. Opposing lawyers will attest to this. So will her sister, an amateur genealogist, who, after tracing the branches of the Towles family tree since its origin, says, "An eccentric crops up every two hundred years."

Although she quickly dismisses the subject, the impression lingers that currently it is Mrs. Root.

Probing and excavating and dynamiting a passageway into her thinking processes was comparable to boring into Fort Knox with a half-inch drill. But I think I finally made it after a painfully slow beginning. We usually started work at midnight and carried on until the hour of collapse—my collapse, not hers. She simply is unacquainted with the meaning of fatigue. Interruptions were frequent. Time after time a telephone call from the jail sent her dashing off like a fire horse.

A national book publisher—of a very conservative house—rejected this book with the note:

"This woman is as large as life and too large for us."

They seemed overwhelmed. This is not unusual. Everyone is overwhelmed by Mrs. Root. She has contributed smoke and fire and vivid color to a profession recognized by all—except those deluded by cinema and television courtroom procedure —as dull and stodgy.

Midway in the creation of the book I remarked to a friend, "Gladys Root has, I believe, won more victories for clients than any lawyer who ever lived."

He replied, "Yes, and a few of them even deserved it."

Mrs. Root would have flared at his sarcasm. She is a great champion of human rights. Her fee is secondary. "I don't speculate on the guilt of a client," she says. "When he comes to me he is innocent, and I'll do my damndest to see that he walks from the courtroom a free soul and becomes, I hope, a good future citizen."

Commenting on lawyers' histrionics, the Supreme Court of Iowa said that it is their honored privilege to:

> "Drown the stage in tears
> Make mad the guilty and appall the free,
> Confound the ignorant and amaze, indeed
> The very faculties of eyes and ears."

This is exactly what Mrs. Root does.

Chances are they won't erect any statues to her after her death; contemporary sculptors would be confronted by a difficult task to chisel those yards and yards of dress fabric. But memories are long-lasting, and her prodigious legal deeds will be etched in the memories of thousands, ranging from the shabby-suited derelicts of life to the moneyed classes who have been touched by trouble. In the turbulent pull-and-tug of the criminal courts, to be represented by Gladys Towles Root is to be certain that you have in your corner a brilliant battler who can influence the odds for acquittal.

Groping for a book title, I telephoned the Weather Bureau to ask if ever a hurricane was named Gladys.

"We're not sure," they deliberated after limited research, "but it would be a good name."

Without reservations, I agreed to that.

Cy Rice

ACKNOWLEDGMENTS

I wish to express my thanks to the following people who contributed their time and knowledge to help me write the story of Gladys Towles Root:

Irving J. Withers, Morris Lavine, Douglas Krumweide, Eula and Lee Thompson, Dr. Jerold B. Rudner, Jim Chown, Frances Murray, Doris Leslie, Lucile Sutherland, Roslyn Wagner, Romeo Carraro, Virginia Bliss, and Nina Quint.

C.R.

Defender of the Damned:
GLADYS TOWLES ROOT

1

PEACOCKS, CHOCOLATES, AND A WOMAN

At precisely 5:55 A.M., Roslyn Wagner, one of three Negro maids staffing a $150,000 Hancock Park, Los Angeles, mansion, came from the servants' quarters, her slippered feet softly padding against the tiled floor of the 75-foot-long lanai. She paused briefly to glance past the sliding glass doors at steam rising from the warmed waters of a kidney-shaped swimming pool.

Entering the completely mirrored foyer, where a waiting client could obtain eighteen separate views of his innocent or guilty face, she ascended the long curving stairway to the second floor, resting a full minute before tackling additional steps leading to the master bedroom.

Her devious journey had taken her past or in close proximity to seven fireplaces, rarely used; six telephones, constantly used; and three color television sets, never used. Her hand twisted the brilliantly sequinned door knob and she pushed silently into the room.

It would be fairly safe to assume that none of the neighbors dwelling in this staid and exclusive residential section start any day in the same manner as the woman sleeping in the king-sized bed in that room. These include Governor Edmund ("Pat") Brown, Normand Chandler, *Los Angeles Times* publisher, Assemblyman Joseph Shell, who was defeated by Richard Nixon in the California State gubernatorial primaries, former Governor Goodwin S. Knight, and Nat "King" Cole.

Décor of the room was lipstick red. The headboard was upholstered in velvet. The long taffeta drapes were drawn. Mirrored tables flanked the bed and two crimson chairs squatted by a mirrored coffee table. The ceiling and doors were gold, the carpet red.

The maid gently touched the shoulder of her mistress.

"Mrs. Root," she whispered.

The cat eyes, that could suddenly change from blue to green to hazel, opened. Long, slender fingers ran through disheveled hair, the color of ripening wheat, which sprawled over the white satin pillow case.

Roslyn crossed to the bathroom. Returning, she handed Mrs. Root a wet washcloth, then a toothbrush holding paste, a bowl of hot water and a glass of tepid water. Ablutions finished, the maid peeled back the bed covers, revealing a tailor-made Empire beaded-at-the-top nightgown with twenty yards of flowing material.

For the next twenty minutes the maid briskly massaged Mrs. Root's feet and legs, then escorted her into the bathroom. While submerged in a tub of hot water, the bather stole periodic glances at a huge office-type electric clock on the opposite wall.

After Roslyn toweled her, Mrs. Root slipped into a long yellow satin robe with broad, deep pockets. Another maid appeared, carrying a breakfast tray containing a hot cereal and a pot of coffee. Mrs. Root climbed back into bed and pressed a button. The bed rose underneath her back, elevating her to a sitting position. An additional button-pushing raised her feet a few inches.

Breakfast finished, she entered the gold sitting room. More than a hundred bottles of assorted perfumes rested atop a broad golden-glassed dresser. She stretched comfortably on

a gold brocaded chaise, signalizing the start of a fashion
parade. For fully fifteen minutes Roslyn carried back and
forth a steady stream of dresses—enough to stock a small
store—from the spacious closets in other rooms.

Mrs. Root kept shaking her head. Finally her eyes lit up at
the sight of a blue peau de soie.

"That's the one."

With it she chose a yard-wide, egg-shaped-crown hat, one
of her own creations, predominantly blue. To pin underneath
the brim, she decided upon a big bouquet of red chiffon poppies. Her shoes were blue, as was her purse. The purse was
adorned with giant red initials. Her jewelry was custom-
made, gigantic, red.

After she finished dressing and came downstairs, the car
was ordered—a black Cadillac Fleetwood, telephone-
equipped, driven by a uniformed white chauffer.

Roslyn inquired, "Anything else?"

"Yes. I'd like to see Chris and Christina."

Roslyn disappeared. A few minutes later shrill cries filled
the house. Two peacocks approached Mrs. Root. She stroked
them tenderly.

"You be good birds," she said softly and promised, "I'll
bring you some nice peaches."

Roslyn coughed discreetly. "And for you tonight, shall
I . . . ?"

"Only if I win," she interrupted the maid's thoughts. A
look of ecstasy flitted over her face and her tongue darted
out, flicking for a split second at her lips.

"How will I know?"

"I'll telephone."

She was referring to a five-pound box of chocolates. There
were always fresh ones around, hidden by Roslyn, their
whereabouts unknown to Mrs. Root. Some in her profession
celebrated their court victories by alcoholic binges or by lowering the barriers on personal vices. Not Gladys Root. She

led an exemplary life: no smoking, no drinking. *Her* weakness was chocolates. But only if her client were acquitted would such indulgence be permitted. This provided a double incentive.

Saluting smartly, the chauffeur held the car door open. Hardly had Mrs. Root settled herself in the rear seat than she reached for the telephone and dialed her downtown office.

"Hello, Jim."

"Yes, good morning."

Jim Chown, her business manager, was speaking.

"Have all the necessary papers packed into a brief case," she instructed. "I'll be there . . ." she consulted a diamond-encrusted wrist watch ". . . in exactly eleven minutes."

"I'll be waiting with them," Chown replied.

The car slowed in front of the ornate fourteen-room ground floor office suite bearing her name upon the purple glass door. Chown tossed the brief case into the front seat through the open window. The car, picking up speed, headed for the Hall of Justice in the Civic Center.

The act rolled back Chown's thoughts to boyhood, awakening memories of trains momentarily slacking pace to take on mail pouches. He watched the Cadillac climb a rise until it became indistinguishable.

Chown, a former engineer, is an astute student of dynamics. Hand him a physics problem on the action of forces in producing or changing their motion, and he'd have the solution with the speed of an electronic computer. There is only one baffler pertaining to physical forces or energy that is unanswerable in his mathematical mind: Gladys Towles Root.

He stood motionless, pondering and marveling. What fueled her system? Was it an unknown or freakish element that flowed into the bloodstream, endowing her with physical endurance superior to that of any man or woman he had ever known? What gave her the surge of power, enabling her to

work twenty hours each day and on a Sunday fly to San
Quentin, Alcatraz or Tehatchapi, visiting men and women
behind the stone walls?

Chown shrugged and gave up.

Tall and regal in bearing, Gladys Root climbed the steps
of the Hall of Justice. She walked with squared shoulders,
poised, her eyes straight ahead as if ascending a throne be-
fitting a queen.

She swept toward the elevators.

Two young lawyers lolling at the cigar stand lowered their
Coke bottles and swallowed fast.

"There she goes."

A little knot of people gathered in front of the elevator
froze at her approach. It was as if they were paying homage
to royalty, granting her undisputed right to enter the elevator alone for a deserved privacy.

"Going up!" called the operator.

The spell now broken, the passengers moved quickly inside, careful not to crowd Mrs. Root, instead squeezing
against each other.

When the elevator stopped she was first off, the other riders
trailing in her wake. The corridor leading to the courtroom
was jam-packed. Only a few were Los Angelenos. Most
were tourists. They had come to watch one of America's out-
standing criminal counselors, who had fought and won more
sex cases than any lawyer in the United States. They had
come to witness human drama, to view the star performer in
a theater of life play her crusading role with a supporting
cast of anguished tragedians, against the scenic backdrop of a
courtroom.

The Junoesque figure was, to moviegoers, a composite of
Mae West and Jayne Mansfield, with a touch of the elegance
and haughty bearing of Grace Kelly. The sultriness of the
voice caused them instinctively to think of Marlene Dietrich.
During the most eloquent and impassioned pleadings, the

voice never roared thunder like those of many of her male counterparts. It was soft and compelling and created sharp, clear images. The voice was a brush in the hands of a competent artist, painting convincing word pictures that hung in the minds of the jury until deliberations.

The voice had no great tonal range, yet it was never dull. It held a dramatic quality generating quiet excitement. And the brain dictating words to the voice was adeptly trained to tear gaping holes in the case of the prosecution.

Why would tourists, whose vacations were limited, be drawn to the Hall of Justice instead of the main Southern California attractions such as Disneyland, Marineland, the Dodgers, the race tracks?

A New Yorker summed it up: "This isn't a trained fish or an animal performing, nor a man-made ride surrounded by ersatz scenery. This is real. Here we have a female Perry Mason . . . a Barnum. And it's all for free! I come to see her legalistic trickery. My wife comes to see her clothes. She never forgot the time Mrs. Root wore a full-length lavender robe and around her neck hung a huge three-foot chain from which a gold crucifix dangled. And her hair! —that was something! She had dabbed it with mercurochrome and purple ink."

He chuckled, adding: "You never saw Leibowitz, Steuer, Darwin, Fallon or Nizer in costume."

Crowd reaction to Gladys Root follows an identical pattern. They don't mob her in the conventional way they stampede to touch a Hollywood celebrity. On the contrary, they break ranks, stepping backward respectfully a few paces for a more extended contemplation. To be too close to Mrs. Root is overpowering; distance lends details.

Unlike Jerry Geisler, famed West Coast attorney, now deceased, who personally handled only cases of the illustrious or moneyed, turning over lesser clients to assistants, Mrs. Root averages seventy-five court appearances per month, de-

fending the little people as well as the big names, non-Cau-
casians as well as Caucasians, and even friends. Friends pay
no fees. Her crowded schedule often requires her to rush
from a recess to plead another case and back again, treadmill fashion.

A tomb-like silence cloaked the crowded courtroom as
Gladys Root entered. A man from Minnesota suddenly
locked tight the jaws that had been working with piston
precision on a piece of gum. The regular cadence of the
asthmatic wheeze of a fat woman from Cleveland subsided.
An Iowa housewife's eyes pinpointed every minute detail of
clothing.

The defendant, a small, middle-aged balding man, the
father of three children, had been accused of child molestation. He rose from his chair as Mrs. Root approached him.
The worried lines in his face smoothed.

He had harkened to the cry of the oppressed: "Get me
Gladys!"

Now he had Gladys.

"Mrs. Root," he asked hopefully, stubby fingers clutching
at her sleeve, "do I have a chance?"

"We'll give them one hell of a fight," she reassured, opening her brief case and rustling through the contents.

At day's end she walked into the Central Market, a block
from her office, and bought ten pounds of peaches for Chris
and Christina. Then she telephoned home.

"We won," she informed Roslyn.

"The candy will be ready."

Arriving home, she changed into a white velvet bathing
suit and, sitting poolside, dangled her long legs in the water,
her purple toenails shining beneath the blue surface. Within
easy reach was a box of candy. After some deliberation she
plucked a creamy nut-topped chocolate creation.

Contentment spread over her face. She chewed slowly,

savoring each bite. A few feet away the peacocks feasted on peaches.

Somewhere in the vast house a telephone jangled, and Roslyn called: "For you, Mrs. Root."

She walked to an extension. "Mrs. Root speaking."

The voice from the Lincoln Heights jail babbled hysterically. When the speaker paused, Mrs. Root echoed the significance of the jumbled words.

"Charged with criminal assault," she repeated. "Don't talk with anyone. I'll be right over."

Again dipping into the candy box, she went into the house, bathed, dressed, poured the contents of two paper packets of gelatin into a glass of cold water, gulped it down, and went to her car.

Destination: Lincoln Heights jail.

Gladys Root was in harness again.

2

PERVERSION AT PAHRUMP

Trial of Leotis E. "Lee" Heater, former Pahrump ranch hand, on charges of "rape, accompanied with acts of extreme violence" will open before District Judge Peter Breen in the Fifth Judicial District courtrooms in Tonopah Monday morning.

The trial is expected to be one of the most sensational in Southern Nevada history. The charge, at the discretion of the jury, carries a possible death penalty, life imprisonment without possibility of parole, or from ten years to life in the Nevada state penitentiary.

District Attorney William P. Beko has indicated that he will ask Judge Breen to exclude minors from the courtroom in view of the lurid nature of the testimony expected.

The defendant will be represented by Mrs. Gladys Towles Root of Los Angeles.

> *Tonopah Times-Bonanza*
> *and Goldfield News*
> September 18, 1959

The only time a person gets up at 6:00 A.M. in Bishop, California—the heart of a sportsman's paradise—is to speed to a supposedly secret rendezvous with an unsuspecting trout.

An exception was Gladys Root. She was getting up to save a life. The life belonged—at least temporarily—to Lee Heater, a slightly built, dark-haired, nervous youth of twenty-seven, whose bluish-white skin coloring strongly hinted of anemia.

Lee Heater was in hot water, scalding water, up to his nostrils. To use a metaphor, he was trying to swim ashore through an angry sea of public opinion. The tiniest ripple might drown him. He trusted that Gladys Root could throw him a life-preserver.

There was a chill in the early morning air as the car bore Mrs. Root and her elder sister, Lucile Sutherland, of Bishop, toward the Nevada state line. The town's streets were deserted save for the lone figure of Jimmy Sargent, of the Water and Power Department, carrying a fishing pole and creel slung over his shoulder. He waved at Mrs. Sutherland.

Mrs. Root's chauffeur was behind the wheel. The lawyer was busily studying a number of notations jotted down in longhand on a yellow tablet.

To their left were the Sierra Nevada Mountains, a granite escarpment whose every rock and rill was explored and made famous by the legendary John Muir, poet and nature lover. Over the "hump" and above the tree line, concealed from view, the rising sun was polishing the tiny jeweled lakes, whose spectacular shores had never been spoiled by discarded beer cans. Crystal-clear, ice-cold streams tumbled from 14,000-foot heights to gurgle under the highway.

Mrs. Sutherland suggested her sister view the magnificence of the scenery. Disdainfully, Mrs. Root shook her head.

"The only scenery I'd enjoy seeing is the smile on my client's face after the verdict is returned."

"It won't be easy," guessed Mrs. Sutherland. She had a superficial knowledge of the case.

"Nothing in this business is."

A chipmunk scampered across the road, barely escaping with its life. The chauffeur, an experienced mountain driver, didn't swerve the car a single inch. After 140 miles of driving they reached their objective: the decrepit outskirts of To-nopah, Nevada, population 1,600, altitude 6,063, seat of Nye County.

"Hungry?" Mrs. Sutherland inquired.

"Nearly always," her sister replied.

Approaching scattered traffic, the Cadillac slowed, turning into the sharply slanting main street, a long and narrow thoroughfare that seemed to be furtively hiding from scattered mining operations on the flanks of steep Mt. Butler on the right and equally precipitous Mt. Oddie on the left.

When the rich silver vein of the Marzipah and Klondyke mine petered out, the town had become a distribution center for machinery, blasting powder, gasoline, whisky and foodstuffs. Spared the fate of dissolving into a ghost town, the pulse of Tonopah was beating faintly.

The sidewalks were weed-ridden and cracked. Some were of board, and at night a loose plank could trip a pedestrian. Many of the buildings had been constructed from jagged native rock. Scores of Tonopah houses had been condemned, pronounced unsafe for habitation because of foundations dug away during boom days.

To the sisters, everything appeared crumbling.

Once it had been different. Tonopah, with its lusty son, Goldfield, twenty-six miles away, attracted—in 1900—adventurers, financiers, miners, engineers, gamblers, journalists, scoundrels—even Wyatt Earp, Tombstone's celebrated sheriff, had come to open a saloon, hoping for a share of the millions in silver being brought to the earth's surface.

Now there wasn't much left. Goldfield was a graveyard of broken dreams. Tonopah was hanging on, daydreaming of a miracle.

So was, at this moment, Lee Heater.

For the first time during the trip Mrs. Root glanced up

from her notes, addressing the chauffeur. "Stop at a restaurant."

"Which one?" the chauffeur asked, perplexed. None appeared appetizing.

"I'll leave it up to you."

The Cadillac—an unusual sight in Tonopah—pulled up before what appeared to be the largest eatery in town. The sisters alighted.

Those knowing Mrs. Root well would have described her attire as conservative. She wore a draped suit with a French hood over her head. Atop the hood was a big sombrero. An antique wooden cross hung from her neck. Circling her finger was a ring fashioned into a cross which had been the property of the Towles family for three hundred years.

From the moment her feet touched the sidewalk she was recognized. The newspapers had announced her coming and the citizens of Tonopah were prepared. Their eyes were slit windows of hate. Their lips were tautly drawn lines of bitterness.

In the beginning, Mrs. Root was unperturbed over the reaction, realizing she was an "outsider" invading hostile territory to do battle. She was aware that even in larger cities the response to a stranger could be uncordial, recalling the San Francisco judge who once lectured to a Los Angeles defendant: "No one from Southern California is going to come up here and get away with what you've done." (Whatever it was that he had done.)

Still, she thought, her eyes sweeping the faces collectively, these people have a different hostility: they resemble a lynch mob.

Lucile Sutherland shivered slightly. "This isn't the way I like men to look at me," she remarked.

"Buck up," Mrs. Root encouraged, pointing out "we're not in Nazi Germany."

"I'd feel a lot safer if we were," Mrs. Sutherland replied.

"The law," Mrs. Root declared, "protects us."

"That'll be a big help after we're swinging from a tree."

Mrs. Root took her sister's arm. "Come on, let's eat," she said, steering her straight toward a group of bitter-faced men loitering around the café doorway.

No one moved to let the women pass. With the aid of her elbows, Mrs. Root cleared a passage toward the entrance. Several men grunted and were observed rubbing their ribs tenderly. The restaurant was empty. Outside, the crowd increased. Periodically they stole glances through the soiled window pane at the diners.

Mrs. Root ordered a steak, Mrs. Sutherland a beef stew. When the dishes of their choice came, they were unidentifiable. Noxious odors rose from the plates.

The sisters exchanged glances.

"Eat your bread and butter, Lucile," Mrs. Root advised. "They forgot to tamper with it."

The preliminary hearing was held in the rear of a store converted into an office for the Justice of the Peace. It was a flimsy building; the words of District Attorney Beko, a well-known local citizen active in civic affairs, carried plainly to the sidewalks.

Soon after Mrs. Root began speaking, a chorus of booing arose from the street. The Los Angeles lawyer paused, her fingers fiddling with the wooden cross hanging from her neck. She tried again, lowering her voice, making certain it stayed within the confines of the room.

"Now, Lee Heater, isn't it true you were handcuffed and your legs chained to a hospital bed . . . ?"

When Lee Heater was in the Army, stationed in occupied territory, the nights were long and lonely and followed a pattern whereby men without women talked of nothing but women. He had two staunch buddies. One of them pinned up photos of ample-breasted movie stars and bragged of his sexual conquests. The other was mono-minded; he was a one-woman man.

The woman was Gladys Towles Root.

He spoke of her, not in a love-starved manner, but with the highest respect, admiration, and regard for her skill and courtroom stratagems. She had successfully defended him against charges of rape and he had gone scot-free.

"I'll never forget her," he recalled. "She marched right up to a husky juror, who was a 240-pound truck driver, and challenged, 'Any time after this trial is over, if you still believe a man can rape a woman while she's conscious, you're at liberty to step into my office and I'll prove that it can't be done.'

"Of course the prosecutor jumped up, yelling objections, which were sustained by the judge. But this didn't faze Mrs. Root. She'd made her point. Then, to drive it still further home, she handed the juror a pencil and held up a piece of cardboard with a hole in the center.

" 'Put the pencil through the hole,' she instructed.

"It was, of course, a variation of the old 'trying to thread the needle' joke.

"The juror tried while she moved the cardboard up and down and from side to side. He failed. Likewise did the prosecuting attorney fail to get a conviction.

"So here I am with you guys, free as a bird and not behind bars," he grinned, concluding with: "If either of you ever has trouble with a girl, remember: Get Gladys."

Never in his wildest dreams had Lee Heater believed the shoe would some day be on the other foot and *he* be scheduled to stand trial, accused of rape, punishable by the death penalty in the State of Nevada. But he never forgot the story or the name of Gladys Root.

That was why he appeared in Mrs. Root's office, accompanied by his former wife, Catherine Hayes of Los Angeles.

Freed on bail, he sought Mrs. Root as counsel. She requested that he make a statement in his own handwriting. When he finished and Mrs. Root read his flow of words, she labeled them as "probably the most fantastic tale I ever heard. An incomparably wild sexual orgy."

In substance, it was:

At the request of Sully Sullivan, a lady friend of his former wife, Heater went to Pahrump, Nevada, to trim trees on the Sullivan ranch. His quarters were a trailer. Mrs. Sullivan received a message that her brother had been injured in an accident. She left, leaving Heater in charge of the property.

His solitary life became monotonous. The ranch was located in rather barren country, with only a few nearby neighbors. Even a car kicking up dust on the unpaved road bordering the fences seemed interesting. He walked to the nearest ranch, owned by Leon Hughes, where he did some sociable drinking, consuming a bottle of vodka.

"I'm a beer drinker," Lee explained. "I'm not used to hard liquor."

The vodka created an awareness of his need for fun and frivolity. Hughes was going to Pahrump, a tiny village eight miles down the road. He gave Heater a lift. At the Pahrump Trading Post Heater ate a hamburger. One of the few business establishments in the village was Jim's Bar. This suited Heater's mood. He went in to do business.

After a few beers, he joined a dice game and in the course of rolling the ivory cubes he was forced into displaying his bankroll. It was sizeable. Tired of gambling and craving a cold beer, he quit the game and lounged at the bar.

Hardly had Heater drained the foam from the top of his glass than a woman slipped onto the adjacent stool. Slowly he swung around for a full appraisal. She was large and reddish-haired, and wore terrycloth shorts. Under the dim barroom lighting, her bare flesh glistened invitingly. Heater was twenty-seven years old, the strange woman many years his senior.

The combination of vodka, beer, and the solitude of ranch living quickly closed the gap in the age differential.

The woman, who gave her name as Maxine Haley, started a flirtation. Heater responded by pinching her leg. She moved closer. He bought her a drink. He ordered another beer. His courage mounted.

He propositioned, "Do you think we could get together and have some fun?"

"Maybe," she replied.

"Come on," Heater entreated, "how about giving a little?"

She shook her head. "Not for nothing."

He was slightly surprised by the answer.

"What's your price?" he asked.

"Ten dollars."

"Fine." The price seemed right.

She said, "Where shall we go? If we go around here I'll have to pay the bartender his cut."

Heater suggested his trailer. She agreed to drive him there. Mrs. Haley told Heater she was on her way to Ash Meadow. He knew that at Ash Meadow was a wide-open house of prostitution under the supervision of a madam.

"You one of the girls there?" Heater asked.

"Only part-time. I live in Las Vegas with my husband and three stepchildren. Every time we have a fight I go there to work. Makes him jealous."

"And this is one of those times?"

"Yes."

Outside the ranch gate she stopped the car. This is great, he thought. All these nights dreaming of a woman and now I have one all to myself . . . no one to intrude. He quickly dismissed thoughts of her as a prostitute by justifying, "a woman is a woman—and I need a woman. Badly."

She turned toward him. "How do you like your sex, Lee?"

Somewhat startled by the question, he was pondering over an answer when she volunteered, "I like mine with a little punishment. Are you game?"

"I—I guess so," he faltered.

"Good," she said. "That's the way you really get your kicks."

"Well . . . I've seen a little of it, but . . . but," the youth hesitated and then went on, "I don't know too much about it."

"You'll learn."

Reaching over, she unzipped his trousers, opened the top button, and demanded, "Give me your belt!"

It was a thick leather belt with a Western-style buckle. He handed it to her.

"Get out!" she ordered.

Heater obeyed, stumbling in the darkness over his trousers, which had fallen down around his shoes. He managed to step out of them. Using the belt for a whip, she began beating him.

"I'm the master," she panted, ripping off his shirt.

She continued bringing the belt downward in savage strokes, lashing him across the back.

"You're my slave," she gasped.

Unable to endure the pain any longer, Heater ran into a little shed used for making wine. There were wooden kegs in the shed and three-quarter-inch-thick rubber tubes used to siphon wine. He hid behind a keg. He felt safe. He could hear her outside calling his name.

At length she discovered him. He had lost the game of hide-and-go-seek-and-beat. Heater grabbed a length of the rubber hose and fought back, striking her many times. She was large and powerful. Exhausted, he fell to the floor; then he got up and they chased each other around the ranch. She caught and tied his hands with the hose and began beating him with a broom handle.

After she grew tired, she released him. Heater, crazed with anger, tried to tie her up. He was now beating her with the broom handle. Periodically she took it away from him. It was sort of a mutual thrashing.

In the barn was a small bed. Both parties, bruised and disheveled and in pain, toppled upon it. Acts of sexual perversion followed, with Heater at one point actually shoving the broomstick handle inside her.

The orgy concluded, Mrs. Haley told him that he had made her realize that she wanted her husband. Heater, himself suffering terrible pain, swabbed her wounds with alcohol. Now, more than ever, he needed a drink of his beloved beer, thinking of it in the sense of a healing balm for his aching body.

After a long search for the car keys, Mrs. Haley drove to Jim's Bar. She cautioned Heater, "You better stay in the car. If we go in together looking like this, they'll know something's wrong and jump all over you."

Agreeing, he begged, "Please don't tell anyone about this."

"I won't," she promised, walking toward the bar.

Heater sat rigid, careful not to lean back and let the seat touch the raw places on his back. Then a thought popped into his mind and it was like a flare that illuminated a pathway to clear thinking: "She'll tell her cronies and they'll come out and beat me up!" One of her eyes was rapidly blackening and this alone, he knew, could touch off a riot.

Leaving the car, he ran to a window of the bar and peeked in. She was clearly discernible, talking excitedly to a group of men. He realized it would be a question of only minutes before they started a manhunt. Noting an old, unoccupied car farther down the street, he fled to it and crouched down on the floor.

The next thing he remembered was hearing a commotion and men's angry voices. One of them was crying loudly,

"Where is that sonofabitch?" The voices came closer. He panicked and ran, the men in hot pursuit.

They caught him. Someone knocked him down. Another stomped him. His memory of the number in the party was vague. He guessed at about four.

He kept shouting, "She beat me . . . she beat me . . . she beat me."

The words sounded unconvincing.

Struggling to his feet, he kept trying to explain what had happened. Jim, the bar owner, intervened and called off the others, leading them back to his establishment.

Still frightened, Heater went to Mrs. Haley's car where he knew there was a canteen of water and, taking it, began the eight-mile walk back to his trailer. He sighed with relief as he plodded achingly along the moonlit road, the lights of Pahrump fading behind. It had been quite a night.

He had no advance hint that the climax was yet to come.

The next thing he remembered was falling asleep in his trailer bed. Over the bed was a small screened window. How long he slept he wasn't sure, but the sound of voices awakened him. He sat up, peering out the window. Beams from flashlights were stabbing the night. They were coming closer.

Although he knew the trailer door was locked, he still didn't feel safe. His nerve-ends were screaming, until he could stand it no longer. He had been sleeping in the nude and he jumped up, facing the square space of window, yelling, "What do you want around here?"

The answer came in the solid form of two shots, aimed by a gunman he identified as lanky, with bushy hair and a green checked shirt. A bullet ripped his abdomen. He gave a startled cry of pain, falling to the trailer floor.

For nearly three days he lay, unable to gain his feet, writhing in a spreading pool of blood. He continually cried for help. The heat under the steel top reached a blistering 118 degrees.

He felt he was going to die, but the will to live was strong enough to enable him to crawl slowly and tortuously about sixty feet to the roadway. Finally a passing farmer stopped his truck, called the sheriff, and Heater was transported to a small hospital in Pahrump, where he remained unconscious for several days.

After Lee Heater signed the lengthy statement, Mrs. Root leaned forward in her chair, gazing intently at him, tapping long fingernails against the desk surface.

"You believe me, don't you?" he asked.

"You're my client."

Heater took a deep breath and said, "I understand under Nevada law I can receive the—the death penalty."

"You can."

He shifted in his chair, crossing and uncrossing his legs.

"How will I make out?"

"That, I believe," Mrs. Root said, careful not to crawl out on a limb that might break, "depends on your lawyer and God's forgiveness."

The accused man stated very slowly and clearly, "I've got the best lawyer and the lawyer is also my God."

A trifle shaken by this expression of confidence, Mrs. Root opened a notebook and said, "Speaking for the lawyer, she will begin your defense by trying to get a few facts straight."

She began questioning him.

As an opening step, Mrs. Root hired two special investigators from Reno to check on Mrs. Maxine Haley, to explore her reputation and to re-enact that evening at Jim's Bar. Next, she was confronted with the difficult task of winning a share of public opinion for her client. Newspaper articles throughout Nevada pictured Lee Heater as a rapist, told of his binding the woman, whipping and torturing her, according to her story. Heater's popularity was reduced to approximately that of a leper attending a health department meeting.

After an operation for the removal of the bullet, the defendant had been transferred to a hospital in Tonopah, where he was treated as a dangerous criminal—handcuffed and leg-chained to his bed. He complained bitterly to both the district attorney's office and the sheriff that he was entitled to an attorney. No one would come forth to represent him.

He sent for the Presbyterian minister of Tonopah, a kindly man with no fixed opinions on the charges. Heater broke down and cried and said, "I want to make a confession."

The minister told Mrs. Root, "I was positive he wanted to admit his guilt. Instead, he said with self-condemnation, 'I allowed myself to become so perverted and lustful that I cheated on the girl I intended to marry.'"

Maxine Haley, who had entered a Las Vegas hospital for treatment, made a voluntary statement to Detective Sergeant Mills and Deputy Marion of the Clark County Sheriff's Office, Las Vegas. It was at variance with the statement of Lee Heater.

She claimed that Heater had been the aggressor throughout; that he asked her to give him a lift to the ranch on her way to Ash Meadow and that there had been no mention of anything other than transportation until they were almost at their destination, at which time he asked: "Would you do me a favor and beat me?"

She contended that it was Heater who made the statement: "I am the master and you are my slave."

He held her against her will, she declared, and twice forced her to have intercourse with him.

The Tonopah courthouse, sitting on top of a hill, is a stone edifice dedicated to justice. A very old structure, it resembles buildings often seen in Western films. The top floor houses the courtroom. The steps are steep. The day of the Roman holiday—the State of Nevada *vs.* Lee Heater—two hundred spectators climbed the weather-beaten steps to scramble for seats.

Inside the courtroom was a pot-bellied wood-burning stove. During cold, wintry days the choice locations were close to it. Spectators were leaning slightly forward—not, as it might be assumed, to catch every spoken word, but because they were occupying old backless wooden benches. The judge entered from a room that looked like an old-fashioned barroom after a free-for-all. He carried an armful of books thick with dust.

A venire had been issued for summoning nearly 120 Nye County citizens for the trial, and from this group nine men and three women were selected to serve. Nearly all the men were farmers. The majority of jurors were middle-aged or older.

Mrs. Root had maneuvered this. "I always try to seat older persons on a jury," she once remarked. "They are more sensible, more understanding, more lenient than the young. They weigh facts, scorning hasty judgment. Because they are older, life is more precious to them and they aren't so quick to decide 'Guilty!' and snuff out the life of the defendant."

Before trial, Mrs. Root fraternized with some of the women reporters staffing the local newspaper and, in pre-trial coverage, her client received a modicum of sympathy. Around town she had become used to walking past scowling faces, but now a faint smile sometimes replaced a former mask of hatred.

Once she heard herself described as "that furriner from California with the big autymobile." Some of the references soon changed to, "There goes that legal lady."

Despite her spadework of good will, the air was still decidedly hostile, and doubts and misgivings tugged at Mrs. Root, seated at the counsel table with Lee Heater. She knew if she took a spectator vote it would be overwhelmingly against her client. Some of those present didn't appear literate enough to count to ten in the proper order, yet seemed fully capable of informing the State executioner the exact weight in grams of the cyanide pellets used in the gas chamber.

She was almost certain of the line the prosecutor's questioning would follow. The line would be straight and unswerving, first building up the credibility of Maxine Haley as a star witness, then concentrating on how innocent womanhood had been defiled. In small Western towns such as Tonopah—as even today in Southern cities—the attitude toward women was that they were never emancipated, and sweetness and goodness oozed from their every pore.

To block any sympathy-gaining moves, Mrs. Root planned to hack away at the reputation of Maxine Haley, carving any virtue she might discover into tiny, irreparable fragments.

From her hospital bed in Las Vegas, Maxine Haley at first had issued a statement in which she claimed she had been attacked by three strange men. Mrs. Root backed her into a corner, finally drawing forth an admission that this was pure fabrication. She resumed the oral bombardment:

Q: Do you reside with your husband?

A: Yes, I live with my husband.

Q: Are you happily married?

A: Yes, I would say so, but I do get mad at him every once in a while. We have our ups and downs like all married people.

Q: Maxine, have you ever been arrested?

There was a slight hesitation and Mrs. Root, sensing the cause of the delay, changed her question.

Q: I mean, here in Nevada?

A: No.

Q: Anywhere else?

A: Yes. (The answer came after a long pause.)

Q: Whereabouts—in California?

A: In Delano, California.

Q: On what charge?

A: I was working in a house of prostitution.

Q: Do you contend that Mr. Heater tied you in a spread-eagle position and raped you several times?

A: Yes, that's right.

Q: Did Mr. Heater strike you?

A: Yes.

Q: Did Mr. Heater say anything while he struck you?

A: All he said was, "Now I am the master and you are my slave."

After court adjourned and Mrs. Root was riding back to Bishop to spend the night, she was searching the archives of her memory, trying desperately to recall where she had read the sentence: "You are the master and I am the slave."

At last it came to her. She called an associate in Los Angeles. In the morning he did some research in the files of the *Los Angeles Examiner*. When he found what Mrs. Root was seeking, he telegraphed the results to her in Tonopah.

She resumed questioning:

Q: Mrs. Haley, do you read much?

A: Sometimes.

Q: What do you read?

A: Generally Sunday School stories.

Q: Did you ever read in the *American Weekly* a story of masochism and sadism as practiced by a tribe of natives in India?

A: Why yes, how did you know?

Mrs. Root described the article to the jury and in quoting the context, referred to "the masters and the slaves." Then she returned to the witness.

Q: Did you intend driving on to Ash Meadow after giving Mr. Heater a lift to the ranch?

A: Yes.

Q: Did you own a tan and maroon overnight bag containing a Sucrets Lozenge box, a green plastic eyebrow pencil, lucite hairbrush, a false teeth denture, powder box and a white plastic comb?

A: Yes.

Q: Then if you didn't intend returning to Jim's Bar after you drove Mr. Heater to the ranch, why did you leave your bag on the bar?

A: I don't know.

Q: Isn't it true you said to Jim, "I'll be back, watch my things"?

A: I guess so.

Having heaped discredit on Maxine Haley as a witness and scored heavily in cross-examination, Mrs. Root called Lee Heater to the stand, confident he would make a good witness.

Q: You told Mr. Hughes, who gave you a lift into Pahrump, that you were leaving with Maxine Haley?

A: Yes.

Q: You told Hughes that you were going to sleep with Maxine?

A: Yes, she was going to drive me home to the ranch.

Q: How many drinks did you have at the bar previous to you and Maxine leaving the bar?

A: I was loaded. I don't know how many she had. I started making passes at her right away and she accepted them.

Q: Did you take a stick or broom handle or something and shove it up inside her?

A: Yes, and she said that felt good.

Q: How long did that last?

A: Not very long.

Q: Did she ask you not to do it?

A: No, she did not say anything.

Q: Were there other acts of perversion?

A: Yes, on the part of both of us.

Q: At any time during the time that you were with Maxine at the ranch did she tell you to take her back to the bar?

A: No, she had her own car.

Q: Have you ever seen Maxine Haley previous to this date?

A: No, I have never seen her before in my life. She said that she ran away from her husband.

Q: Did she say she was going to Ash Meadow?

A: Yes.

Q: Is there a house of prostitution run by a madam in Ash Meadow?

A: I have heard that there is.

Q: Did you receive any encouragement from Maxine at the bar?

A: Yes, very much so. She was all for it. Even when I reached over and grabbed her leg, she got a thrill from it.

Q: Did she return the caress?

A: Yes, and not by just looks, either.

Q: What kind of discharge did you receive from the Army?

A: A general discharge under honorable conditions.

In his closing remarks District Attorney Beko attempted to justify Maxine Haley's profession by contending that every person was entitled to make a living as he saw fit; that in the State of Nevada prostitution was as honorable as any job, for, after all, it is the oldest profession.

"It took a city slicker to come in and take advantage of an unsuspecting woman," he kept emphasizing.

He exhibited photographs of Maxine Haley showing the bruises inflicted. Mrs. Root countered with a set of pictures revealing scars covering the back of Lee Heater.

In her final summation Mrs. Root became a criminal defense maestro, flaying the prosecution and biting into the star witness with words that cut through the air like a steel whip.

"Mrs. Haley is a liar by reason of her having made a number of inconsistent statements. At first she claimed that three men raped her. She stated to police officers that the defendant, Lee Heater, tied her in a spread-eagle position and that he raped her on a number of occasions. We do not feel that after the orgies that took place he was physically capable of raping anyone.

"Also, you will note that after all of the alleged beatings, the 'victim' performed acts that are not entirely consistent with hatred or anger on her part toward the defendant." (This was in reference to certain perversions of sex, admitted by both parties.)

"There is no question that she was badly beaten, as the District Attorney has pictures to prove. However, most of the bruises are on the back of the body, indicating that she voluntarily submitted to the beating by reason of her masochistic tendencies."

Recurringly, Mrs. Root kept asking, to draw attention away from Heater, "Where is the man who did the shooting?" She cried, "Where is the murderer? Why isn't he before you, ladies and gentlemen, the man who attempted to take a life? Has the prosecution made bargains behind your backs? Are they the jury, ladies and gentlemen? Or are you the jury?"

She continued: "The motive in this case is plain. Jealousy. Maxine Haley wanted to make her husband jealous. That's why she was going to Ash Meadow. The Lee Heater incident presented an even greater opportunity. Publicity and notoriety and attention focused on her. And to show him she could get another man.

"Here was a woman many years older than the defendant. All of you know the powers of a woman. A woman can control any sex situation. The male body is susceptible to her charms. A male can be manipulated, his will bent and directed.

"The hand that rocks the cradle still rules the world. And this hand of Maxine Haley undid Lee Heater's trousers and took off his belt.

"Was she not the one who was asking? Was she not the one who was rocking the cradle?"

At this juncture the jury broke into frenzied applause.

Judge Breen hammered with his gavel, calling for a recess.

Mrs. Root was counting heavily on the courtroom conduct of Maxine Haley to help turn the tide in her favor. Caught off guard, Mrs. Haley flirted with men, smoked publicly during the recesses and was noisy. She loved being the center of attention.

When Mrs. Root resumed her argument there was scarcely a sound from the jury or the audience. They sat rigid. Standing before the jury box, the California lawyer asked:

"What would your son have done under the same circumstances?"

Allowing this thought to sink in, her rich voice rose as she said forcefully: "But for the grace of God, there go you or your son."

An elderly man sitting on one of the rear benches sang out, "Praise the Lord!"

Although she hadn't been quite finished, Gladys Root thought it best to close on this outburst.

She sat down, breathing heavily. Perspiration glinted on her finely chiseled features.

Judge Breen spoke to the jury: "The Court instructs the jury that if the jury find the defendant guilty of rape, and find that such rape is accompanied by acts of extreme violence and great bodily injury inflicted, then the jury is privileged to fix the punishment at death."

This was the fourth and concluding day of the trial. It had necessitated hundreds of miles of commuting from Bishop to Tonopah for the trial itself, preliminary hearing, and investigations.

Preoccupied with studying another case, Mrs. Root never left the counsel table. After slightly less than four hours of deliberations, the Nye County District Court jury returned with a verdict of assault and battery. Heater shook hands with each juror.

Assault and battery is listed as a misdemeanor and carries a maximum penalty of up to six months in the county jail or a fine not to exceed $500 or both. Judge Peter Breen sentenced Heater to thirty days in jail and fined him $250.

Heater was happy to the point of being unable to express his feelings in words. Spared from a possible death sentence, his fine was negligible and the jail term would pass quickly.

Within six months the man who shot Heater was tried and convicted.

On the ride back to Bishop, Mrs. Root was strangely silent. Her sister, feeling that she was suffering the effects of a letdown, tried to cheer her up.

She reminded, "Bishop might be a small town, but we have chocolates, you know. You deserve a victory celebration."

"Victory, hell!" Mrs. Root snapped.

Mrs. Sutherland was puzzled. "You saved a man from the gas chamber, life imprisonment, or ten years, and you don't consider it a victory?"

"I do not," Mrs. Root stated with conviction. "I should have got him off."

"But Lee Heater was satisfied. Did you see how happy he. . . ."

"Well, I wasn't," Mrs. Root interrupted.

"Hmm," Mrs. Sutherland mused. "I guess there'll be no chocolates tonight."

"None, Lucile. A few more of these setbacks and I'll have to get all my clothes altered," Mrs. Root mentioned. It was obvious her mind was sloping toward candy.

Recalling her sister's huge wardrobe—the many deep closets crammed with wearing apparel—Mrs. Sutherland whistled softly and said, "That would be the biggest job since building the Pyramids."

3

GET ME GLADYS!

In 1930 Gladys Towles Root, who numbered among her hobbies saving beads, feathers, and strings, was about to embark on a new career of saving: people in trouble.

Impatiently she awaited their arrival.

Freshly graduated from the University of Southern California, and the recent bride of athletic Frank Root, with the ink barely dry on her bar examination papers, she sat, hopes soaring, behind the second-hand desk in her newly-opened law office at the Bartlett Building, Seventh and Spring Streets, Los Angeles. Located in the heart of the city's financial district, the office was a short four blocks' ride in a patrol wagon from Skid Row.

It consisted of a divided cubicle, the square footage comparing favorably in size with the ladies' room in a small town bus station.

Her father had wanted her to become a lawyer.

Her mother had wanted her to be an actress.

This matter would, in the future, be settled by a compromise.

Before Mr. and Mrs. Towles departed on their annual six-month European vacation, they conferred with their daughter. Her father handed her a check, "This money will take care of the rent for six months," he said. "Every young lawyer is supposed to starve to death for the first six months, so don't be discouraged if you follow the pattern."

Kissing her daughter goodbye, her mother offered a modicum of wisdom, "Be broad-minded toward unusual behavior, Gladys. Think of people as loose spokes in the wheel of life."

Out of hearing distance of their daughter, Charles Towles forecast, "She's going to make it, because she's an ambitious fighter."

In one of the divided cubicles, the reception room, the battered typewriter operated by Winnie Dickey was chattering away at a great rate of speed. Unfortunately, this close friend and part-time secretary was not preparing briefs or torts—she was merely practicing typing. But the sharp sound of the keys striking against the aged Underwood's platen and bouncing off the walls of the oppressively hot room was sweet music to the young lawyer's ears.

She was dreaming . . . and waiting . . . and dreaming.

They were lofty dreams, beautiful gold-tinged fantasies. Each was individually shaped into the physical form of a client eagerly paying an enormous stipend for her services. Each was a famous person. Each resolved into a case resulting in quick acquittal. Each brought showers of accolades from the defendant, the press, the judge, and even reluctant ones from the district attorney.

Yet even dreams have time limitations. After five hours they were beginning to fade.

Arriving at her office that first morning she had sat and sat and sat. Fearful of missing a client by lunching out, she gobbled a sandwich and apple she brought from home. When, on rare occasions, the reception room door opened and closed, her spirits rose only to plummet upon hearing the voice of a mailman or solicitor. Just one person had entered the inner sanctum: a building maintenance man checking the lights.

She was growing restless. Crossing to the open window,

she peered down into busy Spring Street, momentarily toying with the idea of sailing a paper airplane constructed from a sheet of her first business stationery. Its descent would be irrevocably bound up with her shattered castles in the air.

She wondered what legendary lawyers such as Arthur Garfield Hays or Max Steuer had thought of on their first day of practice. Surely they must have had at least one client.

She realized that her surroundings were, to any possible client, not very confidence-building. If more than one person entered the office it would be crowded. The room temperature was a high broil. The air-conditioning was manually operated: an opera fan belonging to her mother was waved to and fro by Mrs. Root, feebly circulated the suffocating air. Five minutes in this steam cabinet, and the client who demanded a jury trial to fight what he believed to be an unjust traffic ticket might wilt until he resembled a person struggling for his life on the witness stand.

On the optimistic side, the worn covers on the law books could build the confidence of a client, for their dog-eared condition engendered a strong belief they had been read again and again. Actually they were purchased at a used book store. For cash.

Her father had constantly drilled into her: "Never buy on time. Only for cash. Or don't buy."

This business principle had paid off handsomely through the years for Charles Towles, the Great Depression failing to scar him noticeably. The majority of his holdings were in real estate that weathered the financial storm.

Laughter exploded from her as she thought, "At least this office is too small to misplace anything in." Miss Dickey appeared, a worried expression lining her face. She looked inquiringly at Mrs. Root.

"Anything wrong?"

Mrs. Root shook her head. "Nothing. Just unwinding. The laugh you heard was not hysteria."

Apparently satisfied, the secretary returned to her desk and resumed typing practice.

Only two pictures obstructed the bareness of the walls of Mrs. Root's office. She was apathetic toward pictures and that morning had pontificated to Miss Dickey, "I have definite objections to pictures hanging in a law office. I feel that a client must have complete privacy with the person who is counseling. Absolutely no distractions. Some unknown person peering at him from a canvas over his shoulder could give him a guilt complex. Or a pretty scene might set his mind wandering."

Miss Dickey nodded and Mrs. Root continued: "Even a diploma or a calendar can distract. These influences make it difficult for the attorney to know the individual immediately. The attorney can't analyze as swiftly. Do you see my point, Winnie?"

Whether or not she did, Miss Dickey's head bobbed up and down. Mrs. Root was a complex character and it would necessitate a life-time of study to understand all her mood variations, whims, conjectures.

Today, in her present lavish fourteen-room suite the walls are bare of pictures. Flowers take their place, both real and artificial. Some are in vases held up by the arms of cherubs.

"Babies or children," she points out, "inspire innocence. Flowers tranquilize."

Still the fact remained that two pictures decorated the walls. They were original oil paintings, a gift from a friend. In deference to him she had put them up. One was a stormy seascape, the other a pastoral scene—a broken-down wagon on a country road and a farmer with a shovel over his shoulder about to remove some of the load from the vehicle.

The friend had said they were symbolic, that her career would probably be turbulent as the ocean and her legalistic work would lift tremendous weight from troubled people.

The opening and closing of the outer door jarred Mrs.

Root from her reveries. She heard a foreign-accented voice saying, "I want to see the lawyer lady."

Smiling widely, Miss Dickey poked her head in.

"Give me a few minutes," Mrs. Root whispered.

The moment Miss Dickey disappeared, Mrs. Root made a quick decision. She took down the two pictures, turning them face toward the wall. Glancing hurriedly into a compact, she applied a light touch of lipstick, smoothed her hair. Her heart was pounding.

A small Filipino entered and timidly approached her desk. She indicated the only vacant chair. "Sit down, please."

He dropped into the seat, faced her, waiting.

"You wish representation?" she asked.

He answered, puzzled, "All I want is help, lady."

"That you shall receive," Mrs. Root assured him.

The man gave his name as Louis Osuna. "I have a wife. I have children. My wife has a husband. She has children."

This was becoming slightly confusing, but Osuna clarified the situation. "She has also other men."

"Infidelity?"

"She go out with them."

"That's infidelity."

"Whatever you call it, lady lawyer," the little man said sadly, "I want divorce."

Before Mrs. Root could promise that she would do her best to secure one for him, Osuna said diffidently, "I—I can't pay you much," a statement she was to hear repeated innumerable times her first few years of practice.

She told him that money was of no concern. What chiefly mattered to her was that she had a client. A real, live client. The first. Joy vibrated within her. She summoned Miss Dickey, who took notes. Finished, Osuna rose to leave.

"Just one more question," Mrs. Root said. "Who recommended you to me?"

"You mean—you mean . . ."

"I mean," she guided him, "who sent you in to see me?"

"No one."

"No one?"

He shrugged. "Well, you see it's hot out. I come into building to get in shade. It's nice cool inside. I think better when cool. I begin to think I need divorce. I read names in directory. I see word 'Attorney.' I come to you. I do something wrong, maybe?"

"You did something right, Mr. Osuna," Mrs. Root told him. "Now you go home and don't worry. You'll have your divorce fast as possible. I'll be in touch with you."

Mrs. Root and her secretary exchanged smiles as Osuna left.

"Winnie," the lawyer said, "we're in business."

Twenty-four hours had barely passed when Mrs. Root received a telephone call from her client asking if he would have to wait much longer for his divorce. She informed him that the first steps were already in preparation, but it took time, and pacified him by stating, "The wheels of legal machinery turn slowly, Mr. Osuna."

The following day, Mrs. Root opened a telegram which read:

AM IN LOS ANGELES COUNTY JAIL. PLEASE COME SEE ME.

LOUIS OSUNA

She dashed over to the Hall of Justice in the Civic Center. It was her first visit to a jail. She felt important, wire in hand, as she presented her credentials at the desk and received a pass.

A deputy sheriff halted her. A veteran of the department, he was a hard-bitten man. In his lifetime he had faced all types of criminals, come up against every conceivable lethal weapon. He was certain there was nothing left under the sun capable of startling him.

He was wrong.

Mrs. Root was wearing a suit made by her mother—the

identical one that had caused a furor at the California State Bar examinations. It was a dressmaker suit with draped coat and tight skirt copied from a European pattern. She wore high-heeled slippers and large jewelry and carried an over-sized purse. Upon her head at a jaunty angle perched a derby hat belonging to her father, who had worn it while marching in a parade for Woodrow Wilson the day he was elected President.

"Wear it and you'll have good luck," had been his advice.

The pungent odor of liberal dabbings of Christmas Night clung to her. Mrs. Root was crazy over perfumes.

Hands on hips, the deputy examined her with jaundiced eye. After a penetrating study that seemed to imply that all freaks were not in circuses, he demanded, "What do *you* want?"

"I came to see a convict," Mrs. Root answered.

"A convict?" The deputy's eyes stopped darting over Mrs. Root's clothing, coming to rest on the derby hat.

"Yes, a convict," she repeated.

For a full minute the deputy didn't speak, finally breaking the silence with, "Are you the lawyer?"

"Yes, I think I'll be."

The deputy said, "Well, he isn't a convict yet—but I don't think it's going to be very long if you represent him."

The prophecy of doom shook Mrs. Root's composure. She sighed. It was comparable to the sound of air leaving a punctured balloon. Upon recovery, she thrust forth her jaw and her credentials.

"Wait here," the deputy advised, handing her a visitor's slip to fill out.

He returned and beckoned to Mrs. Root. Following him, she entered a room with three tables and a guard rail in the center. Seats for prisoners were on the inside, visitors on the outside. Osuna was seated, waiting for her. She sat down next to him, wondering why so many blue-coated policemen were ringing her.

Someone tapped her sharply on the shoulder. Startled, she looked up at the deputy.

"Madam," he addressed her, "you're sitting with the prisoners."

Attempting to conceal her embarrassment, she jumped to her feet, changing position to the visitors' side of the guard rail, and began questioning Osuna.

"Tell me what happened."

"I come home. I see a man getting in bed. He. . . ."

"Your bed?" she interrupted.

"My own bed. With my own wife."

"Go on," she urged.

"They didn't hear me come in. So I sneak out again. I go buy gun and come back. He sees me, grabs his trousers, jumps out back window. I shoot at him." He paused for breath.

Mrs. Root asked, "Did you hit him?"

"No, I miss."

"And?"

"Then I shoot her."

Whistling softly under her breath, Mrs. Root asked, "What is the extent of her wounds?"

"To big extent."

"How big?"

"To extent she now dead," Osuna related.

From simple divorce the case had suddenly changed to murder.

Osuna stated flatly, "I do it because divorce take you too long."

"Too long?" Mrs. Root repeated, bewildered. "You only came to see me yesterday."

"I know, I know," Osuna agreed. "But you say, 'The wheels of legal machinery turn slowly.' So I decided to speed them up."

Mrs. Root said, "You went about it the hard way. It's murder now. Murder, you know, can cost your life."

"Not if you good lady lawyer," Osuna grinned. "You ever lose a case?"

"No," she answered truthfully.

"Good," Osuna said happily. "I tell all prisoners in jail about you."

Louis Osuna was returned to the Tank, where the so-called riffraff of Los Angeles were incarcerated awaiting trial. The atmosphere was anything but antiseptic. The air was stale, combining the noxious odors of a slaughter-house, poolroom, and gymnasium. Drunks, too ill to stand on their feet, slumped against the cold concrete floor. Morals offenders and thieves were regular tenants and a smattering of feeble-minded prisoners gibbered incessantly.

Standing in the middle of this den of caged human animals, Louis Osuna proclaimed in a loud and clear voice, "I got a wonderful lawyer."

The room grew silent. The majority of these unfortunates would plead guilty, falling upon the mercy of the court; a few would be represented by the public defender.

"Does he want money?" a hoarse voice boomed.

"It's a she," Osuna corrected. "I don't think she cares about money."

A raggedly dressed prisoner with a face like broken pavement raised himself partially off the floor and called, "What's her name?"

"Gladys," Osuna told the listeners.

Veterans of the Tank who had been accustomed to accepting any sentence the judge meted out began showing interest. They grouped around Osuna, plying him with questions. Why anyone would stoop to defend them was a baffling enigma.

"Maybe she needs practice," a sex deviate suggested.

"I'll give her all she can handle," a voice piped up. "Every month. Regularly."

A tall, thin man, badly in need of a shave, struggled to his feet. His manner and bearing were faint reminders of a past dignity. Because of a vocabulary far exceeding that of his fellow inmates, he was known as "The Brain." His talent as a pickpocket had endowed him with a position of leadership. His opinions were widely sought and respected.

"What do you think of her?" he was asked.

"I think," he replied, "that the lady in question is a humanitarian."

"I don't getcha," said a vagrant with seven convictions, "but I like the sound of the word." Cupping his hands against the sides of his mouth, he shrilled in a whisky-cracked falsetto: "Get me Gladys!"

Others took up the cry, chanting, "Get me Gladys!"

Several jailers appeared, attempting to quiet the tumult by shouting, "Shut up, you bums! Go sleep it off!"

When order was restored, one of them turned to another and asked, "Just who in the hell is this Gladys?"

"I never heard of her," was the answer.

It wasn't long before he would.

The seeds of publicity planted by Louis Osuna began sprouting, coming up as human vegetable matter, recognizable as derelicts from the Tank. Fifteen of them sought her counsel that first month.

Her father had erred in his prediction that she would starve to death. While few of her clients paid for her services with money, some discharged their obligation by bringing her chickens, ducks, and geese, causing her girlhood friend Doris Leslie—presently a Los Angeles ballet teacher—to remark, "It was hard to tell if Gladys was in the livestock business or running a Skid Row mission."

Unless she diagnosed them as chiselers or phonies, Mrs.

Root never turned a client down. Fast becoming expert at character appraisal, she seemed to have a knack of instantly spotting the undeserving. With those she wasted no time, dismissing them with a terse, "Sorry, I will be unable to handle your case."

Her steadfast refusal to squander even a minute of precious working hours was one of the props upon which her legal business was secured, enabling her office in the years ahead to handle more criminal cases than any other private firm in the United States, plus a sprinkling of divorce, paternity, domestic, accident and civil matters. Specializing in morals cases, her office defends 1,600 accused per year.

The clients who began streaming into her office caused her to wonder: Why did they seek her?

She asked them; the answers were similar. No one would take their cases. They could pay nothing, or at best a token fee. Not only did most lawyers dismiss such cases as impossible, but generally they felt that defense of a morals charge was detrimental to their reputations.

These considerations failed to deter Mrs. Root. Such people touched her heart, tugged at her emotions. She seemed bound by a sense of duty to help them. "I never could resist the plea of a person in trouble," she said compassionately.

A chip off her mother's philosophy was applicable to her fundless clients: "No matter where you plant the seed of good, it may not come up in the soil at once but the pollen from its flower might be blown many miles away—and in the long run be beneficial."

Her background was indisputably upper-class. She had viewed the world through rose-tinted glasses equipped with built-in blinders shutting out sordidness. Few of the members who moved graciously in her well-bred social circle faced up to reality. Her parents' wealth and position blacked out intimate acquaintance with the "other half."

Before entering law school her concept of a trial was

colored by fiction. Courtrooms were perpetually character-
ized as arenas of combat, where duels took place between
brilliant prosecutors and defenders. The fate of a man or a
woman was decided by sudden surprises, silver-tongued
oratory, legalistic wizardry—all coming under the heading of
law—a cartilaginous structure that holds mankind together.
The guilty would die or be confined to a square of concrete
for x number of slow-passing years. For the innocent the
delicate scales of justice tilted favorably, permitting them to
walk into the bright sunshine of freedom.

Murders, robberies, swindles were the headline grabbers
. . . the black ink devourers . . . the giant type consumers.
These were the sensational trials that sold the newspapers.

But what of the others—those rating a short paragraph in
the press, or more often no mention at all—who were now
clogging her office? These were the little people, the unfortunates without money, without reputation, many without
pride. They were misfits unable to conform to the conven-
tions and pressures of the world. Some were mentally ill and
their only help was psychiatric.

In overwhelming numbers they sought Mrs. Root. They
could not afford those champion defenders of human rights
whose fees were astronomical and whose records of victories
were nearly unbroken.

These were the cases that launched her. They caused a
metamorphosis in her thinking. Here was where she lost her
baby teeth, acquiring in their place a sharp set of bicuspids
and molars conditioned to shredding false evidence. Here was
where the girl became the woman. She cared not if her
clients were panderers, prostitutes, procurers. Each person,
she contended, was entitled to choose his legal representative.

How long it generally takes and how many hard knocks are
required to learn compassion cannot be gauged in hours,
days or years. To some, that knowledge never comes. Mrs.

Root's eyes were opening wide to view a new world almost faster than she could assimilate its implications.

She had to talk with someone who might be able to understand and advise her in her bewilderment—to shed some light on her new thinking. She telephoned Morris Lavine, an attorney with a reputation for fairness and principles. Lavine later was to try sixteen cases before the United States Supreme Court.

They met at lunch. Lavine kidded, "Is our young tyro setting the legal profession on fire?"

In her rich voice she replied, "I'm not even kindling the smallest flame."

"Discouraged?"

"I'm puzzled, Morris."

"Well, bare your soul," he encouraged.

"I'm sure my discoveries aren't new to you," she began. "There's a certain class of people not being properly defended. They're condemned at the moment of arrest. The true circumstances aren't always understood."

Lavine played with a butter-knife, turning it over and over in his hand. "You mean, like sex deviates."

"Mostly. There's a glandular situation here. Physical disturbances. Mental conditions. Often borderline cases. Some are framed. A lot of them are convenient victims—even the victims of children. They can't fight back. Am I boring you?"

"Not a bit."

"I want to help these people, Morris."

Lavine said, "I agree they need it. It's a noble idea, but what about profit?"

"You mean making money?"

"That's the general conception I had in mind."

"The hell with the money!"

The food arrived. Lavine nibbled sparingly. Mrs. Root

started her fork toward her mouth and then lowered it again. Her appetite had vanished.

Lavine posed what he considered a loaded question but one whose answer might help him understand this idealistic young lady better: "Do you believe that you're defending criminals?"

Her spine stiffened and her eyes blazed. "Decidedly not," she snapped. "You know what makes a criminal?"

"Suppose you tell me," Lavine suggested.

"It means being caught at a crime. Nothing more. It makes me boil when I hear anyone referred to as a criminal. Many people walking the streets are far greater criminals than those who are doing time."

Lavine nodded, "I'll agree to that," he said.

"I don't want to sound like a missionary," she said, "but there are so many people who need help who shouldn't be shunted aside."

Lavine suddenly asked, "What is your strongest belief in life?"

"That God is love," she answered without hesitation.

"Any other beliefs?"

"The Golden Rule."

"Can you stick to these?"

"I can," she answered.

He looked at her searchingly, asking, "Do you mind if I tender some advice?"

"That's the main reason we're having lunch."

"Okay, Gladys. Here it is: Never go into any judge's chambers alone!"

"Why?" she asked, puzzled.

Lavine, lowering his voice, leaned toward her. "I don't mean to cast any aspersions on the bench, but consider this: you're an attractive woman, and beneath the robes of a justice there does exist a man. Always have an opposing lawyer or another lawyer along for any meetings. Keep aloof. Then nobody will ever be able to point a finger of suspicion at you."

Thirty years later, after Mrs. Root had severely drubbed a male prosecutor, the defeated lawyer bumped into Morris Lavine. Still reeling groggily from defeat, he asked, "What's this woman got besides the fancy hats?"

"Flair, style, judgment and skill," Lavine reeled off.

"That's all?"

"Apparently it's enough," Lavine replied.

Lavine and Mrs. Root had offices in the same building and they walked back together from that luncheon meeting. As they entered the elevator, he said in a low voice, "Keep up your convictions and never compromise them. Above all, don't let the legal profession change you."

"But will I," Mrs. Root asked him, "ever do anything for the legal profession?"

A smile tugged at the corners of Lavine's mouth as his eyes examined the bizarre clothing she was wearing. He replied hedgingly, "Keep trying. You may not dignify the profession, but you'll certainly pump some life into its tired old arteries."

Before Louis Osuna was scheduled to appear, Mrs. Root tried several other cases. Her debut involved a young man accused of robbery. Judge Charles S. Burnell announced to the jury:

"This is Mrs. Gladys Towles Root, attorney for the defendant. It is her first case."

She won an acquittal for her client. In retrospect, Mrs. Root remarks "It must have been out of pure sympathy for a very nervous woman."

On the heels of this initial victory came a case involving a morals offense. Her client was charged with molesting a six-year-old youngster. He was 76 years old, a pensioner who acted as a baby-sitter before that term was coined.

Mrs. Root worked hard, delving meticulously into three

backgrounds: the defendant, the mother of the child, and the child herself. She couldn't afford investigators, and to pay for the services of a psychiatrist—or alienist, as they were then popularly called—was out of the question.

The defendant, she learned, had raised a fine family and had been a success himself. It was illogical, she theorized, that he would suddenly degenerate into a sex criminal. She found he exhibited symptoms of senility, which seemed to reduce his mentality to that of the plaintiff.

Placing the mother of the child on the stand, Mrs. Root completely discredited her.

"You asked the accused to come and sit with your daughter nights?" Mrs. Root began.

"Yes."

"Why did you have to go out nights?"

"I work during the day. It's warm where I work. I like to go out at night, take a walk, get the fresh air."

Mrs. Root strode to the counsel table, dug into a brief case and brought forth a piece of paper which she consulted and carried back to the witness stand. She could easily have memorized the contents, but felt this lent authenticity.

"Is there something fresh about the air in Jack's Bar?" she flung at the witness.

The witness gasped. Before she could reply, Mrs. Root rattled off: "Or the Cozy Corner? Charley's Tavern? The Idle Hour? Or Dew Drop Inn?"

"I—I only had a beer in those places," the witness protested.

Mrs. Root surmised, "The amount of alcohol you consumed is of no concern, but evidently it was more important than staying home with your child."

The child was cross-examined. She was a pert, redheaded youngster with the kind of blue eyes fiction writers are apt to describe as "innocent."

Mrs. Root started slowly. "Are you a good girl, Nancy?"

"Yes, I'm a good girl."

"Do you know the difference between good girls and bad girls?"

"Yes."

"Good girls," Mrs. Root explained, "tell the truth. Bad girls tell lies. By a lie I mean a story—something they made up that didn't really happen. Will you, Nancy, tell me the truth so you can be known as one of the good girls?"

"Yes."

"Now think carefully and tell me the truth. Have you ever played with yourself? Down below? Touched yourself?"

The prosecutor bounded to his feet objecting. The objection was sustained.

Mrs. Root tried again. "All right, Nancy. Tell me then if you've touched other little boys and girls in the neighborhood and let them touch you?"

This time the judge overruled the loud objections.

The child hesitated. Tears were forming.

"Come on, Nancy," Mrs. Root pressed. "The truth. It's important to tell the truth."

"Well . . . I. . . ." Her voice trailed away.

"Have you, Nancy?"

"Well . . . just a little," came the admission.

Mrs. Root changed her line of questioning. "Do you know a man named Tom Blake?"

"Yes."

"You didn't like him, did you?"

"No."

"Was he a bad man?"

"Yes, he was."

Mrs. Root reminded, "He played with a little girl . . . a little girl about your age, Nancy. And you know what happened to Mr. Blake, don't you?"

"I—I don't remember."

"Think, Nancy. Think back."

"I don't remember."

"He went to jail, didn't he?" Mrs. Root prompted.

The child remained silent.

Mrs. Root raised her voice. "Didn't he?"

"He went to jail," the child admitted.

Again Mrs. Root went to a new subject. "Do you like ice cream?"

"Yes, ma'am," she said eagerly.

"Candy?"

"I do. Yes."

"Does your Mama give you an allowance each week?"

"A what?"

"Does your mother give you some money each week? Money to spend on anything you like best—such as candy and ice cream?"

"Yes, she does."

Mrs. Root asked, "How much does your mother give you each week?"

"Fifteen cents."

"Each week?"

"Yes, each week."

Moving closer to the child, Mrs. Root sought her eyes, holding them. "Do you know an ice cream and candy store near your house called The Sweet Shop?"

"Yes."

"Do you know Mr. Gordon, the owner?"

"Yes."

"Does Mr. Gordon tell the truth?"

"Yes."

"Mr. Gordon, who tells the truth," Mrs. Root said, "says that some weeks you spend as much as two dollars buying ice cream and candy in his store. Now Nancy, if your mother only gives you fifteen cents each week for these things, where did all this money come from?"

"I—I don't know."

"Did you find it?"

"No. I—I just had it."

"Nancy," Mrs. Root's voice grew stern. "The truth is that you did have it. But you got it from [name of accused]. Isn't that right?"

Sobs shook the child.

Mrs. Root reconstructed. "You remembered the man you didn't like—Mr. Blake—who went to jail for doing something naughty . . . for touching a little girl. So you told [name of accused] that you'd say he did the same thing to you." She paused, then continued: "Unless he gave you money from time to time."

Tears streamed down Nancy's cheeks. Mrs. Root extended her handkerchief. The child wiped her eyes, blew her nose.

"That's the truth, Nancy. The truth. You know it's the truth," Mrs. Root hammered relentlessly.

"Yes, yes, yes," the child blurted.

The case against the unjustly accused man came crashing down. Petty blackmail, performed by a child, had been revealed.

Actually, there is such a dearth of cases where a lawyer's stratagem wrings admissions of guilt from flustered witnesses, breaking them to complete confessions, that a trained researcher might have to hunt through trial transcripts for years before uncovering any. A well-coached adult witness doesn't crack like the six-year-old interrogated by Mrs. Root. Most of the confessions can be seen and heard only by moviegoers or television viewers. In them the clever lawyer has the wavering witness in a high state of confusion, until, hopelessly trapped, he shouts, "I killed her!" and the judge pounds his gavel, shouting "Order in the courtroom!"

In the thirty-three years during which Mrs. Root has defended all types of criminals she has savagely attacked the testimony of State witnesses. A unique description of her trial tactics was furnished by Tom Cameron, former veteran court reporter for the *Los Angeles Times.*

"Where I live," Cameron recalled, "was a cat who had a litter of kittens in the back yard. A peculiarity of female cats shortly after they have kittens is that they attract the tomcats, although they have no use for them. This stray tom came around. The kittens were in the yard underneath flower bushes. The female was up in a tree, purring off-key love calls which translated might have meant, 'Come on up, let's have some fun.'

"Tom climbed the tree. The female, backing away slowly, led him out on a limb. In a split second, when the unsuspecting tom was off balance, the female flicked out a paw to send him flying to the ground.

"The act made me think of Mrs. Root in the courtroom, doing—in a manner of speaking—the same to those under cross-examination."

The Louis Osuna case was another triumph. He was found guilty only of manslaughter, receiving a sentence of ten months.

A few months after the Osuna trial—in 1931—Mrs. Root scored what she considers the most important conquest in her entire law career. A male Filipino and a white woman stood before her, announcing they wished to get married. Mrs. Root quickly detected that the girl was pregnant.

"We have come to you," the darkskinned youth said, "because a Filipino and a white woman are not allowed to marry in the State of California. We do not think it fair. Can you do anything about it?"

"I will certainly try," she told them.

She began research, quickly finding the barrier, a decision handed down by a Los Angeles Superior Court judge: "Filipinos are Mongolians and thereby cannot marry with Caucasians."

Her first step—for the record—was to escort the young

couple to the marriage license bureau, where authorities refused to issue them a license.

Then Mrs. Root delved into genetics, eugenics, the study of races. She learned that the Philippines and the people of the Philippines were included in the term "Asiatic," and since the term "Mongolians" applies to all of Asia, the Filipinos are therefore included in the category of the word "Mongolian" and for that reason cannot be lawfully married to Caucasians in the State of California.

She discovered that the Legislature, in constructing a law prohibiting the marriage of these parties, did not construe that the Malay race was included in the category of Mongolian.

Mrs. Root contended that the Filipino race is a race by itself, distinct and entirely apart.

She took the issue to a higher court, and won a victory of paramount interest and vital concern to every Filipino in the State of California. All Filipino-Caucasian marriages since 1929 were now held binding, and the legitimacy of the children of such marriages was thereby recognized.

All restrictions were lifted.

Mrs. Root received accolades from the Filipino press. Benigno Cortez, Managing Editor of the *Los Angeles Call*, termed Mrs. Root "brilliant" and wrote, "She defended with dramatic power and impressive sincerity the cause of the Filipinos."

4

THE SHORT POLITICAL LIFE
OF GLADYS ROOT

By the time the elder Towles returned from Europe, their daughter was wallowing in cases. Dozens of clients were clamoring for her services. They queued up at her office door. The seediness of their clothing might have suggested to an observer that the Main Street Mission had opened a branch in the Bartlett Building.

Gladys Root needed larger quarters. She needed another secretary. She also needed money.

Although the volume of business was overwhelming, paying clients were alarmingly rare. Mainly, her cases were charity. A large number of these had been referrals from the City Mothers' Bureau. She was swamped, working harder than a doctor in the midst of an epidemic.

In his customary fatherly manner, Morris Lavine said, "Gladys, you've got to attract some paying clients."

"Just how do I go about it?" Mrs. Root asked.

An idea formed in Lavine's mind. "Getting into politics might be the answer."

"On which side?"

"The Republican," he said.

"Why the Republican?"

"They've got more money."

"I'll give it some thought," she replied.

She promptly joined the Junior branch of the Republican Study Club of Los Angeles. Attending her first meeting, she observed that the members ranged in years from their mid-fifties to octogenarians. Although celebrating only its first birthday, the organization was lifeless, threatening to die on the political vine.

They were sorely in need of a youth movement; Mrs. Root was the answer. She moved in and seized the reins of leadership. She soon became president.

In her acceptance speech she avowed, "We will build an organization as healthy looking as Herbert Hoover's cheeks." His cheeks were full and rosy in 1930, not yet sallowed by the effects of the national depression.

Younger members were sought, with an object of forming a national organization to assist in the campaigns. They aligned themselves through the Women's Republican Study Club. Something was needed to spark enthusiasm and raise money.

Taking the bull by the horns, Mrs. Root proposed a reception in honor of President Herbert Hoover. "Everybody will turn out to shake the hand of the President," she predicted, adding: "and we'll sell lots of tickets."

The applause of the meeting was thunderous. She was given carte blanche to manage the entire affair. The bottom of the treasury barrel was scraped, and Mrs. Root was handed the money, which she took to a printer.

The invitations read ". . . in honor of the President of the United States of America, Herbert Hoover."

Proudly she showed one of them to her mother. The response was a stifled scream as the alarmed parent blurted, "Gladys! You're going to jail!"

Jails held no terror for Mrs. Root. She asked, "Why, Mother?"

"Because you know he isn't coming," was the simple answer.

Mrs. Root counteracted with a defiant, "Well, I didn't say definitely whether he was or not."

Mrs. Towles collapsed into a chair. She was not a believer in smelling salts, but this was one time when she could have benefited by a few sniffs.

"You *know* that he isn't coming," she stated categorically.

"He *was* invited," Mrs. Root reminded her mother.

Response to the invitations was overwhelming. Additional printings were necessary. Money rolled in. Ticket demands were heavy. There was even some scalping.

No one doubted that the President, along with Mrs. Hoover, would appear.

Press and radio interest snowballed. Firmly in the center of the vortex, Mrs. Root posed for news photos, made speeches, spoke over various radio stations.

Then panic seized her. She sought attorneys George Bush and Joe Scott, bigwigs in West Coast Republican party politics.

"Is Mr. Hoover coming out?" she demanded.

They both said not to their best knowledge.

"I sent a wire to the White House secretary," Mrs. Root said.

Bush asked, "What have you heard?"

"Nothing."

Bush and Scott traded blank looks and both shook their heads negatively.

Addressing Bush, Mrs. Root said accusingly, "You're the manager here and you wanted the Juniors to do something, didn't you?"

"They certainly seem to have done something—possibly more than they can take care of," Bush said acidly.

Mrs. Root spun on her high heels and walked away.

The Hollywood Knickerbocker Hotel, site of the affair, began telephoning Mrs. Root. "We have far more reservations than the banquet room can handle," the manager related.

"Use the entire lobby then. Rope it off," she ordered.

Mrs. Towles asked her daughter, "Aren't you even going to have somebody stand in for the missing President?"

"We can't very well get a wax figure from a museum," snapped Mrs. Root.

To thwart what might be the beginning of a lively argument, Mrs. Towles changed the subject by inquiring, "Have you decided what you're going to wear?"

"No, mother."

Mrs. Towles noted it was five-fifteen. "You're due at the reception at six-thirty," she said and mused: "Let's see—that will barely give me time enough to make you a dress."

Mrs. Root kissed her mother. "Make a sensational one, Mama," she encouraged. "I'm going to take a bath."

Before she could run the water the telephone began jangling. The police and sheriff's office wanted to give the President and Mrs. Hoover the necessary protection and security. The newspapers began demanding the exact time of the President's arrival. The Hollywood Knickerbocker asked the same question.

Mrs. Root had a stock answer: "I haven't as yet been advised of the President's arrival."

Meanwhile Mrs. Towles was working feverishly designing a long evening gown created from two hand-painted lace tablecloths recently bought in Belgium. The dress was literally pinned on. Mrs. Towles was ingenious at draping. A few pins and a prayer later the dress was finished.

"I keep feeling it should be a shroud," she commented mournfully, assisting her daughter into the dress.

Mrs. Root, accompanied by her husband, began the drive

to the Hollywood Knickerbocker. Traffic was jammed three blocks from the hotel. Her husband, waving a press pass like a magic wand, opened a pathway. Inside, Mrs. Root pushed through the throng toward the speakers' table. The questions hurled at her were divided into two sets of inquiries: "When are the President and Mrs. Hoover due?" "What's the name of your dressmaker?" The assemblage grew impatient. The cookies and punch had run out long ago. It was a worried Mrs. Root who called the meeting to order. Her thoughts dwelt on mob violence and on Juanita, a woman of questionable reputation during the gold rush days. Juanita was hanged from a tree. Nervously Mrs. Root arose to speak, deciding to make a clean breast of the entire fiasco.

Straight toward her at that moment came a uniformed Western Union boy carrying a yellow envelope. All eyes focused on him. He handed the wire to Mrs. Root. Ripping it open, she raised her hand for silence. When the murmur of voices died she read into the microphone:

"Thanks for the great honor extended to me and Mrs. Hoover but we regret that we cannot be with you tonight.

Herbert Hoover"

The crowd was placated.

A representative of the Republican Central Committee delivered a verbose speech paying homage to the President and Mrs. Hoover, and Mrs. Root concluded by reading a telegram she composed stating that the Junior Republican Club was grateful they could entertain in his honor.

The crowd went home happy.

Mrs. Root telephoned her mother, who said, "You were lucky. People were very kind to you this time, but please, please, Gladys, never pull another stunt like this."

As it happened the affair was a germ that spread, to be later adopted by the Democrats, thus giving birth during the

Roosevelt regime to the hundred-dollar-per-plate dinner honoring FDR.

"And he never appeared either," Mrs. Root defended. It wasn't until nearly two years later that Mrs. Root inadvertently learned her mother had contacted a friend in Washington, D.C., who had sent the telegram supposedly from the President.

After complete recovery from the close call, the lawyer plunged even deeper into her political work. The Junior Republican Club was requested to send a representative East to a political meeting in Washington. Mrs. Root was voted delegate—to travel at her own expense.

Eager to expand, she suggested to her club that at the Washington meeting she propose the organization become national. Members unanimously backed the idea; also her recommendation to transport a crate of oranges back East to give away to women delegates. Mrs. Root arranged through an orange grove association to secure the fruit.

Airplane travel was still in its infancy in 1930. That left two choices of transportation—train or bus. Members of the Junior Republican Club would be at the station to see her off—so the train was a must. A transcontinental train trip in those days was a status symbol. Only one problem confronted her: she didn't have sufficient funds.

She solved the wardrobe question in a hurry by packing her honeymoon clothes, supplemented by some knitted dresses she finished in a single day, using extra-long fat needles while she interviewed clients.

With little money in her purse, she boarded the train at the Los Angeles Union Station. From the rear platform of the observation car, Mrs. Root made a short speech, waving goodbye to the crowd gathered to see her off. Alongside her was the crate of oranges.

Her train ride was short—sixty miles. She alighted at San

Bernardino and bought a bus ticket to Washington. Boarding the bus, she argued with the driver.

"We can't transport those oranges," he said firmly.

She frowned, insisting, "You have to. They're part of my baggage."

The driver flushed and said, "There'll be no oranges on this bus."

Mrs. Root took a firm stand. "Then," she said, "this bus isn't going to leave."

"Listen," the driver was beginning to shout now. "This is a big company and no one person is going to hold up departure."

"A big company can be sued," she warned.

Changing his tone, the driver pleaded, "Please, lady. I've got a schedule to make."

"And I've got a convention to make."

Ignoring her, the driver called "All aboard!"

Mrs. Root stood in a position that blocked the door from closing.

"Move, lady!" the driver ordered.

Folding her arms defiantly across her chest, Mrs. Root was adamant. "I'll move whenever you decide to take the oranges aboard."

The enraged driver sputtered and finally, unable to put his thoughts into the proper words, capitulated. "Okay, okay," he sighed. "I'll take your lousy oranges."

As the bus, now behind schedule, took off, the driver, glaring into the rear-view mirror at Mrs. Root, muttered, "I'll never drink orange juice again the rest of my life, so help me."

Fifteen miles from the nation's capital, Mrs. Root alighted —with, of course, the orange crate—and purchased a train ticket to Washington. Arriving in style, she checked into the Willard Hotel, occupying the smallest and cheapest room. The orange crate filled nearly half of it.

The next day she attended the first session of the meeting. Ten minutes after the meeting was called to order the Chairman made a statement with which Mrs. Root was in complete disagreement. The tall Californian rose.

"Mr. Chairman!"

Locating the source of the voice, the Chairman, before recognition could be given, asked the designation of the speaker.

"Gladys Towles Root, Junior delegate from California."

"Juniors," the Chairman answered in a modulated tone, "were called back here to be seen and not heard." Then he trumpeted, "You're out of order!"

Gladys Root, shoulders squared, marched stiffly as a drilling soldier straight up the aisle and out of the auditorium. A terrible thing had happened. She had been denied the right of speech.

Back in her hotel cubby-hole she hastily stuffed her belongings into suitcases as she solemnly pledged to the empty room, "I am hereby and as of now, finished with politics forever."

She telephoned for a bellboy to bring up a dolly. The orange crate was loaded upon it. She directed him to take the fruit to the office, where she told the startled manager, "These are for your hotel with the compliments of the Junior Republican Club of Southern California. Serve them to anyone you wish."

"Even Democrats?" asked the grateful manager.

"Preferably," Mrs. Root said.

Her political career was terminated.

5

THE ROOT OF ALL LEGAL

Whenever things lag at the Hall of Justice the boys in the press room, bored with waiting for some newsworthy happening, introduce a controversial subject: Gladys Towles Root.

Inevitably, questions fill the air. Why does she dress so startlingly? Why does an aura of sensationalism surround everything she does?

Around the civic center she is nicknamed the Lady in Purple.

After one of her courtroom appearances, a reporter—wishing his wife was around to aid with the description—wrote, "She appeared in iridescent taffeta of blue and pink, an ankle-length gown with a tight waist and huge billowing skirt, very Victorian. She resembled a middle-aged princess in a Victor Herbert operetta."

Her bizarre taste in clothing and jewelry, plus an offbeat matching personality, makes Mrs. Root one of the most widely discussed individuals in Los Angeles. When she shops, crowds form. At first there are giggles, snickers, laughter, at her clothing. Then there is always someone who explains who she is and the gathering stands in silent awe. Heads nod in recognition and the women who were standing transfixed press forward to see for themselves what she buys and to examine what she is wearing.

She commands the respect of her colleagues. Mrs. Roslyn Goodrich Bates, a Los Angeles attorney now deceased, said, "Mrs. Root is very competent and very thorough. She doesn't need to be exotic in her clothes. She has enough ability without it. In one jury case she changed coats three times in one day. I've worked with her on various organizations and women lawyers' groups, heard her lecture to women's clubs, and she's one of the hardest working women I've ever known."

She is so notorious in a city of millions that a man dialing Information asked for the number of Gladys Root and without a second's hesitation the operator asked, "Do you mean Gladys Towles Root, the attorney?"

No one has ever claimed Mrs. Root wears "a dress." Whatever she appears in is labeled a costume.

Roby Heard of the now defunct *Los Angeles Mirror-News*, in a three-part story on Mrs. Root, agreed with Mrs. Bates. "Mrs. Root," he wrote, "doesn't need these eccentricities of dress. She has enough on the ball to carry her cases without coming to court dressed like a peacock from another planet."

Averaging seventy-five courtroom appearances monthly, she is fantastically garbed for each. To repeat the same dress would be the equivalent of committing a cardinal sin. She favors black Chantilly lace, multi-colored sequins, pink ostrich plumes, red suede, various shades of velvet, woolens adorned with dozens of ermine tails.

Her hats are gigantic. A trial judge once ordered her to remove one. She did, and exposed the court to hair done up in pin curls.

"Put it back on!" His Honor shouted.

Skirts favored by her range from skin-tight to yards and yards of ruffled petticoat. Her hair has been dyed green, pink, lavender, mint, magenta—every color in the rainbow.

She's experimented with laundry blueing, cake dye, and a special mercurochrome-and-violet-ink job.

Despite her flair for the melodramatic, Gladys Root is a distinguished and respected member of the bar, a most sought-after lecturer and fluent banquet speaker.

Outspoken against society, she characterizes it as cruel and ridiculously stupid to punish a man for an act arising from neurotic upbringing or faulty glands.

"Rather than jail these offenders, later to release them in a more dangerous condition, science should be given an opportunity to cure them," is her contention. She is a strong believer in administering psychiatric examinations to those reportedly victimized by a sex crime.

"The victim often has deliberately invited the attack or actually been the aggressor," she affirms, adding: "Contrary to popular thinking, even children are capable of being the aggressor in a perverted relationship with an adult. Also, a shockingly large number of disturbed teenagers will frame adults."

She can cite cases that she has tried and won in which girls of six, eight, ten and eleven years provoked assaults upon themselves.

Her stoutest feelings regard rape. "Only one out of a hundred of these cases is founded on fact. The woman usually gave willing consent, fabricated the story, or encouraged the act," she professes.

Mrs. Root's favorite pastime is sniping at antiquated statutes that outlaw "unnatural" lovemaking between husband and wife, mentioning, "I can recall dozens of cases where husbands were arrested on these charges. Fortunately, I saved them all."

She is also diametrically opposed to laws providing punishment for homosexual acts between consenting adults. Likewise to laws against prostitution.

During 1959 she tried nine murder cases, five of them

women charged with killing husbands. All were acquitted. Recently she opened the trial of a client charged with murder and closed it with a ninety-day jail sentence for assault.

Her annual gross income runs into a high six figures. Today, many of her clients are wealthy, and for them her fees are substantial. Of those in the lower income brackets who seek her, many are Mexicans and Negroes. Never forgetting clients serving jail sentences, she corresponds with them and often drives on holidays as far as 500 miles to keep in touch and buoy up their hopes.

In Los Angeles County, where 239 communities search for a sanity infringed upon daily by contrived publicity productions, residents' skins have been pricked by so many sensations that it seems fairly safe to assume that the antics of a downtown woman lawyer would be nearly obscured. Nothing could be more incorrect. Mrs. Root has never been upstaged by Hollywood.

Kendis Rochlen of the *Los Angeles Times*, in a column called "Candid Kendis," commented: "The Hollywood dolls may think they're pretty good at making eye-catching entrances in breathtaking outfits but they're all pikers compared to a gal who operates in our downtown courtrooms.

"She not only wears clothes you see from a distance but hear—try swishing twenty yards of taffeta in a skirt, plus sixty yards of ruffled petticoat up a narrow courtroom aisle sometime. With Gladys it's one extreme or the other. Clothes are either a Cinemascope production or so tight she can barely mince along. Same with her hats. They fit tightly to her head like a second skin or they have the wingspread of a DC-7. Her jewelry looks too big and too bountiful to be real—but real it is."

One Sunday Mrs. Root strolled along fashionable Wilshire Boulevard and left the local populace gasping. Her hair was dyed a vivid pink, and matching that color were two lambs on a leash. The lambs bleated, pedestrians and car drivers stared. Alcoholics Anonymous gained several new members on that memorable day.

Various newspaper and magazine writers have turned their analytical prowess upon Mrs. Root, probing for clues to her behavior. Barely able to puncture the surface, they generally have been forced to improvise with scores of adjectival descriptions.

They tell you she wore a topaz pin the "size of a breast shield," and an amethyst ring "having the dimensions of a golf ball," or "large brooches made into earings."

But they fail to tell you *why*.

When Gladys Root is asked the direct question, "What makes you like you are?" she'll say, "I'm a little nuts, I guess. I missed my calling. I should have joined a circus. I'm a screwball."

Those knowing her intimately will dispute this self-analysis. They will tell you that she's an uninhibited woman who finds an escape from the morbidity of her sex-crime cases by running wild in clothing and jewelry tastes. They will also tell you that the frustrated actress in her rears up as often as possible.

The woman is full of surprises. One evening she gave an elaborate party at her home. At 11 P.M. the doorbell rang and Mrs. Root, after collaring the guest of honor, went to answer it. There stood her uniformed chauffeur with a skunk on a leash. The skunk, attired in formal dress, wore a cape and a jeweled collar—although few of the guests were able later accurately to describe the animal's outfit.

The instant reaction was to retreat in panic.

There is an anecdote illustrative of the preparations made by Mrs. Root, when she faced a problem. For several years, she had been taunted by a Los Angeles judge who at each annual Criminal Bar Association party flung the challenge,

"If you'll jump into this swimming pool, I'll do the same." As at most California parties the pool was omnipresent.

Each year the identical challenges and dares were hurled. They got under her skin. She decided to do something about it. The first step called for a consultation with Eula Thompson, her modiste.

Mrs. Root appeared the evening of the party in a stunning gown. The judge found her standing at poolside. "Come, on Gladys," he flung down the gauntlet. "I'll jump, if you'll jump."

He had expected her to cringe and move away from the pool's edge.

Instead she gave the judge a push. He hit the water with a resounding splash. Then she jumped in. Standing in the pool, shoulder-height in the water, she peeled off the specially-made evening gown in a quick-zippered lightning change. The gown had a separate skirt, fastened in front with three hooks and easily removable, as were the sleeves.

Climbing out, she went into the house and changed into another dress she had brought with her. The astounded judge went home to dry clothes, and failed to reappear at the party.

Mrs. Root doesn't always provide the surprises. She received a jolting one herself the day she visited her favorite jewelry store to shop for a necklace. The proprietor greeted her and then his face blanched.

"Would you be kind enough to step into my office?" he requested.

Expecting a private showing, she followed him.

Closing the door, he asked in guarded tones, "Where, if I may inquire, did you purchase the diamond pendant that you're wearing?"

"Oh, this," she said, highly pleased, fingering the exquisite jewel. "A client I defended sent it to me yesterday."

The jeweler stared at the pin. "You say you defended him?" he repeated incredulously.

She nodded. "Yes, on a burglary charge."

"Was this the man I read about in the newspapers who was accused of stealing the [   ] collection?"

"Yes."

"How many years was he sent up for?"

Mrs. Root replied, "He didn't go to jail. We won an acquittal."

"All I can say," the jeweler said, "is that you must be quite a lawyer."

"Thank you," Mrs. Root returned.

"Because," the jeweler went on, "the pendant you have on *is* from the missing [   ] collection."

The color faded from her face. "Are you—are you sure?"

"I am certain, Mrs. Root."

Before the end of the day the pendant reached its rightful owner.

Few persons know of the time petitioners rang the doorbell of her Muirfield Road mansion. Representing the Hancock Park property owners, they wanted her to sign a paper to prevent Nat "King" Cole, the Negro entertainer, from buying a residence in this exclusive neighborhood.

Mrs. Root fixed the group with a frosty stare. Without permitting them inside the house, she delivered a little speech.

"Gentlemen," she said icily, "if I signed this petition I couldn't live with myself. We accepted Negro blood in transfusions to help save our country during the war, which thereby assisted us as individuals, and if we accepted their blood we can do nothing else but respect them in every right we can give them. To live in any place they choose constitutes one of those rights."

She had one final sentence for this group whose proposal

bulged with signatures and who thus far had encountered no opposition:

"Furthermore, I have strong doubts of the legality of such a petition."

The Bureau of Internal Revenue once disputed the amount of tax deductions made for Christmas gifts. Christmas in the Root manse means stacks of boxes that would fill an average-sized house from floor to ceiling. Caught up in the holiday spirit, she becomes a walking Santa Claus. The decorations in her house stagger the imagination.

Focal point is a black Christmas tree. The base is covered with chicken-wire backing with black cloth on the front. Lights show through it. The tree itself is hung with clusters of artificial purple grapes. Placed in a crossfire of dark blue and red lights, the grapes seem to become fluorescent.

Every friend—and their number is legion—receives a gift. This includes police officers and court house employees, starting with those holding the lowliest jobs. The list runs to numerous pages.

When the Internal Revenue men questioned many of the items—particularly why so many cases of whisky were dispensed—Mrs. Root, far too busy to go into the matter in detail, argued the legitimacy of the gifts and said, "If you dispute these, set a reasonable figure for what you'll allow on the total gifts."

The spokesman for the government shook his head. "That will be impossible," he said.

Mrs. Root's cat eyes flashed warning signals. "Have it your own way, then."

The Bureau investigators began gathering up their papers, happy with the easy victory they had scored.

Then Mrs. Root casually dropped a bomb: "But if that's the way it's going to be, remember this: Hundreds of bottles of whisky were given away—one bottle at a time. And that's how we'll go to court and try the case. One bottle at a time. I'm going to appeal every last bottle of it."

The Government settled its case.

About fifty guests vividly recall a birthday party she gave. A week prior to the affair she telephoned her modiste.

"Can you come over tonight and plan something with me, Eula?" she asked. "I want to discuss a full-dress suit and an evening gown. They're not for me."

Mrs. Thompson asked who they were for.

"For two pigs," came the information.

It was a strange answer, Mrs. Thompson mused. She had never known a single instance when Mrs. Root had been sarcastic or rude. When she arrived at the Muirfield Road house she learned to her surprise that the clothes *were* for pigs—real pigs. Also jeweled hats. Unbeknown to the guests, the pigs were coming to the party.

Mrs. Root discussed the animals' apparel. Mrs. Thompson went home to begin work by conferring with her husband, Lee. There were certain imponderables. How long should the legs be? How large were the pigs in circumference? What did they weigh?

Lee suggested his wife call Mrs. Root, find out who owned the pigs, and telephone him. The man's name was Fred Parsley. Mrs. Thompson contacted him.

"My name is Mrs. Thompson. I'm a dressmaker and I'm making a suit and a dress for the two pigs that Mrs. Gladys Root is getting from you. I. . . ."

"You're what?"

"Now don't hang up, Mr. Parsley," Mrs. Thompson said hurriedly, claiming, "I'm not insane. I haven't been drinking. Believe me, please, I. . . ."

"Goodnight, Mrs. Thompson."

"Please, Mr. Parsley," she pleaded. "Please hold on just a minute."

Finally the owner of the pigs was convinced of the validity of the call. He said they weighed around fifty pounds each and furnished, to the best of his knowledge, the other measurements.

The chauffeur was instructed to give the pigs tranquilizers before making an entrance with them. In doing so there was a case of mistaken identity, and one pig received both doses. The drugged animal soon fell asleep near the cocktail bar, but the other became overly active, almost breaking up the party.

There was the time a major motion picture studio, wanting to familiarize one of its fading stars with courtroom procedure and protocol before she played the role of an attorney, sent her to Mrs. Root for coaching. She was to be paid handsomely for the lessons.

The star had been told that the lawyer was somewhat of an actress herself, and instructed to emulate her as much as possible. Mrs. Root talked on techniques, but her pupil had other ideas, fluffing off most of the advice.

Finally, disgusted, Mrs. Root sent her back to the studio. Calling them, she told the director, "Never mind sending me a check. I can't teach this woman anything."

Soon afterwards, the seer of Hollywood—Jeron King Criswell—in his syndicated newspaper column "Criswell Predicts," forecast that a story based on the career of Gladys Root would, in the future, be filmed.

"I know one actress who'll never get the job," she said.

Mrs. Root decided after her first brush with the celluloid world that it was far easier to tutor her own clients in histrionics than teach professionals. Only once did she come a cropper: the day Pauline Le Roy, accused of white-slave charges involving three young Los Angeles girls, fell prone to the floor with a loud bump.

Judge R. H. Scott requested: "Counsel, in the future I wish that you would advise your client not to faint in court." To which Mrs. Root commented after court was adjourned, "It's seldom you run up against a judge who lacks appreciation of the theater."

She has received both cold stares and compliments from various judges before whom her cases are heard. One of the highly respected veterans of the bench, Judge Leon Yankwich, called her into his chambers after Mrs. Root had managed to get a counterfeiter off with a light sentence. He complimented, "I've never seen anything so beautifully handled in my life. I have always wanted to meet you and work with a woman who wears the clothes you do."

There were two Los Angeles judges who forbade women to appear before them with hats on. Consecutively Mrs. Root drew them. Sans hat, she feels naked, besides being deprived of one of her greatest pleasures in life. At a meeting in the chambers of one of these magistrates he remarked, "I see that you're not wearing one of your famous hats today!"

"I respect the wishes of the Court, Your Honor," she answered.

After studying her for a moment, he asked, "Isn't it a bit unusual for you to pay any attention to what somebody else wants?"

"Yes, it is," she said frankly.

The judge then asked if she ever felt uncomfortable in her unconventional clothes.

"Never," she said. "These are my working clothes. If I wore the sports dress or tailored suit that the average person wears, I'd be miserable. I couldn't do my best. I have to have color and distinctive style. I like everything that's very feminine and luxurious looking. And different."

Impressed by the honesty of her answers, the judge said,

"Well, I'll waive my request. After the noon recess you may bring your hat back from the office."

"Thank you," Mrs. Root said, "but that won't be necessary. I have one in a box under the counsel table."

The other judge, Allen W. Ashburn, failed to rescind his ultimatum. This caused a furor. Women and men attorneys and judges alike said they had never before heard of a judge enforcing such a rule, and they formed into two hostile camps of opinion.

Superior Court Judge Georgia Bullock, only woman jurist on the superior bench, thought the order a good one, even though she had never heard of it being enforced before.

"Personally, I think it is better not to wear a hat," she stated. "That was my own practice when I was an attorney. I think there is a formality which is more fitting if the hat is not worn."

Judge Bullock said a picture hat or other such headdress on a woman lawyer might tend to detract from legal proceedings, declaring, "Her manner of dress should not be a matter for fashion inspection during a trial."

Kathryn J. McDonald, president of the Women Lawyers' Club, said it was the first time she had ever heard of a "no hat rule" for lady lawyers.

"It might be very inconvenient for someone making several court appearances," she said. "It's no fun taking your hat off and putting it on and trying to keep your hair straight. However, a judge is the boss in his own courtroom and is entitled to make rules he feels will be conducive to dignity.

Kenneth E. Lynch, past president of the Los Angeles Lawyers' Club, said he thought the rule was "ridiculous." Present President Percy Hammond agreed. "I am greatly surprised. I have never heard of such a rule," he commented.

Neither had Julius V. Patrosso, president of the California State Bar. "It might be one judge's idea, but I never heard of it in any rule book," he added.

Selma Moidel Smith, president of the Southern California Women Lawyers' Association, expressed the opinion, "It's a matter of personal concern for the Court. Women often feel that a hat is more formal and wearing it shows greater respect for the Court, because they feel they are better dressed."

Mrs. Root was not exactly inarticulate on the subject, pointing out that women advocates in French courts wear special hooded robes and spend much time in beauty parlors acquiring a hairdo which will go properly with the hood.

"If we're going to require a formal dress for women lawyers, let's agree on what it should be and provide proper checking facilities," she advised. "However, I think a woman is not properly and formally dressed unless she has hat, gloves, and purse.

"I also think that respect for the Court is created by the judge of the Court himself and the atmosphere of judicial dignity rather than the attire of any lawyer."

Gladys Root is a composite of four distinct personalities:
The actress.
The attorney.
The nonconformist.
The woman.
The nonconformist showed itself early in her life. One of her first rebellious acts occurred at school when at the age of nine she fought for the right to dress as an individual. She disagreed with an order to wear a uniform: middy blouse and blue serge skirt.

"Why should everybody dress the same?" she demanded, rising from her seat in class.

The teacher, unaccustomed to opposition from the youthful mind, was nonplussed. "Because—because it's a rule," she tried to explain, and reminded her, "You'll have to obey it."

"I'll obey it," returned the little girl, "but that doesn't mean I'll like it."

The teacher sighed. "Now can we consider the subject closed and get on with our geography lesson for today?"

Remaining on her feet, Gladys asked pointedly, "Aren't teachers supposed to set an example for the children?"

"Why certainly."

"Then why shouldn't the teachers wear this school uniform?"

"Africa," the teacher began, "is a continent. . . ."

Gladys sat down.

Being forced to wear the school uniform and dress just like the other children rankled little Gladys. A week later, still frustrated over her inability to fight the measure imposed upon her, she walked home from school with her friend Doris Leslie. It had been raining for days and the earth resembled a gooey chocolate pie.

On a hilltop washed clean of vegetation, adobe mud glistened. Adobe, as most Westerners know, has clinging qualities much like those of plaster. She looked at Doris. Doris looked at her. Words were unnecessary. They climbed the hill. Gladys scooped up a fistful of mud, drew back and pushed it onto Doris' cheek. Doris squealed delightedly and retaliated. Before long the pair appeared to be wandering fugitives from a minstrel show.

They experienced sheer, untrammeled joy. Gladys felt particularly exhilarated. Subconsciously she was protesting the wearing of the school uniform, and each time she decorated the face of Doris she was defying school authority.

Before they reached their respective homes, the mud caked and hardened. It was with some difficulty that Mrs. Towles recognized her daughter. After the bath came a sound spanking. Her bottom stinging, she telephoned Doris.

"It's hard to sit down," she told her friend.

"For me too," Doris said.

Gladys, mulling the situation over, replied, "You know, I think we put the mud in the wrong place."

Her irrepressible spirit grew ever livelier. While her cooking class was making dough for bread one day, the teacher had to leave the room for a few minutes. Upon returning, she was aghast to see dough hanging from numerous places on the ceiling.

Horrified, she demanded, "Who did this?"

Gladys confessed.

The teacher fought for self-control. "You have," she asked gravely, "a reason for your actions?"

"Oh, yes," the child spoke up. "I did it to help me remember my lessons."

An explanation was requested.

She launched right into it. "You see, yesterday you told us about caves. You said that stalactites and stalagmites were in caves. One goes up. The other hangs down. I get 'em mixed. By throwing the dough and watching it hang down, I'll always remember now which is which."

Gladys Charlotte Towles was born September 9, 1905, the day California was admitted to the Union. Place of birth was a two-story frame house on a six-acre wheat ranch, now a part of downtown Los Angeles. She was the second daughter of Charles H. and Clara Deter Towles. Charles was the son of English immigrants. The couple first met in Topeka, Kansas, where Clara worked as secretary to the Speaker of the House in the State Legislature.

Moving to Los Angeles in 1892, Charles Towles became supervising agent for the Singer Sewing Machine Company. His ambition was to become a lawyer, but he was forced to drop out of school for financial reasons when his first daughter, Lucile, was born in 1895. He permanently retired from business at the age of fifty-five.

From the time Gladys Towles attended Hoover Elementary School, through her years at Los Angeles High School and the University of Southern California, amateur dramatics and clothes played important roles in her life. In the beginning she staged shows in the Towles barn, graduating to the Community Players of Hollywood. Although the casts were sometimes paid for their efforts, her parents forbade her to accept any money.

Brilliant colors always fascinated her. One Fourth of July, while her father slept, she painted his car red, white, and blue. As her father trembled with anger, Gladys reminded him, "Daddy, it's the Fourth of July, you know."

"At least it proves you're a patriotic American," the elder Towles said, gazing sorrowfully at his car.

At parties, Gladys could be relied upon to make late and eye-filling entrances. Her costumes were spectacular. These were usually created a bare three or four hours before their debut. Twice, the speed of assembling them, combined with daring originality, nearly had disastrous results.

Her senior year in high school, she attended a graduation party held on the beach at Santa Monica. She yearned to wear something that was really different. Rummaging around, she uncovered some gray Angora yarn. In something less than three hours she knitted a short bathing suit with a little pair of panties. It fitted perfectly, but she needed some kind of a foundation underneath.

Her mother had just bought her sister a silk vest. This, surmised Gladys, was the answer. Sneaking into Lucile's room, she filched the garment and sewed it into the knitted bathing suit. She fastened artificial flowers to the waist. On her head she wore a big straw sombrero with real flowers.

Her attire made as big a splash as the waves and she pranced down to the water's edge with the compliments of her classmates ringing in her ears. Placing her hat carefully on the beach, she dashed into the surf and dived under an incoming breaker. When she surfaced, she felt something strange happening to the bathing suit. The spaces in the knitted fabric, formerly no bigger than an eighth of an inch, had expanded to a full inch or more, and the suit, instead of being up around her thighs, now stretched down to her ankles.

Because of its sheerness and fineness, the silk vest was cut to shreds by the salt water. She stood helpless, and what had been previously a bathing suit was now something indescribable, wet, clinging, and only partially covering her. Anyone with the dimmest of eyesight could peer through the holes. She attempted to pull the sad suit up protectingly, but the weight of the water dragged it down again.

The entire beach reacted hysterically. Finally, a gallant boy came running to her rescue with a blanket.

She had still another escapade involving her wardrobe in an effort to come up with something unusual for a high school dance. It all started when she noticed an apricot tree in the backyard. She stood entranced, an idea forming; she would cover a dress with the fresh leaves.

The spring foliage had just burst into its loveliest and the leaves were pretty and alive and green. Picking the leaves at sundown, Gladys washed them carefully, polished them, and put them in the ice box for stiffening purposes. She appropriated one of her sister's best slips. Using little pins supplied by the Singer Sewing Machine Company, she made a gown with one leaf pinned atop the other. To complement it she stripped an old hat and created a new one with small pink roses.

From two in the morning—the time she stole the slip—until six, she labored.

The less her mother knew of it the better, after a tragedy of a few weeks before. *That* was the time she had decided to make an evening gown from the beaded portieres that divided the parlor from the dining room. It seemed a sound plan, but the moment all the beads were hooked on the dress the threads broke and what were formerly portieres became a pile of colored beads on the floor.

The day of the party Mrs. Towles asked what she was

wearing. "It's a surprise," her daughter answered mysteriously. "You'll love it."

When Gladys slipped into it, Mrs. Towles agreed she looked ravishing, but asked with concern, "Will it stay together?"

"I'll take my chances," her daughter replied.

If the dress created a sensation upon her entrance, it was destined to provide an even greater one as the hour approached midnight. The action and the warmth of dancing were too much for the leaves, which began to split away from the pins.

Then the leaves came tumbling down!

As Gladys rushed from the dance floor, a friend caught up with her, thrusting a dress into her arms. "Your mother gave it to my mother to give you just in case of an emergency," she panted.

Gladys seized it gratefully. "The emergency is here," she cried, sprinting for the protection of the ladies' room.

After a few years, when paying clients began to find their way to her office, she bought a car, a convertible. The top was rarely up. An extremely competent driver, she paid scant heed to speed laws, racing through the streets with her long hair streaming behind her in the wind. In her exotic clothing, strollers must have thought a multi-colored comet was streaking along close to the earth.

Chief companion on these wild jaunts was Douglas Krumweide, her personal hair stylist. Krumweide was far braver than the average man. He was also more thankful. At the conclusion of one of these mad jaunts he would slowly descend from the car to bend over and kiss the ground.

After three speeding tickets, a judge sermonized, "Los Angeles is a growing city which is rapidly becoming populated by a migration westward. Those who seek to take up life here shouldn't become so badly frightened that they return where they came from. I appeal to you for the safety of all pedestrians and motorists in Southern California to strongly consider giving up driving a car."

She never drove again.

Mrs. Root seemed to thrive on danger. An example was what happened after she tried a case in Bakersfield, assisted by a colleague, Herbert Grossman. Krumweide had accompanied them. After dining at the Saddle and Sirloin Restaurant, it was time to fly back to Los Angeles in a private single-engine Beechcraft she had chartered for the round trip.

They hailed a taxi. As Krumweide opened the car door, a large mongrel dog jumped in.

"Leave him or her or it be," Mrs. Root said. "Not every stray dog is allowed to ride in a taxicab."

To their amazement, when they reached the airport the dog ran straight to their plane, jumped onto a wing, and leaped into the cabin. The passengers followed. Mrs. Root sat with the pilot; Grossman and Krumweide occupied the rear seat. It was Grossman's first flight.

The night was beautiful. Stars studded the sky and the moon was yellow and full. The plane gained altitude, rising over a barrier of mountains. Below was the treacherous Ridge Route, graveyard of truckers.

Suddenly the dog's spine stiffened until the animal seemed made of marble. A few seconds later, without even a warning splutter, the motor died. The pilot began calling the nearest airport—Palmdale—to "Get the crash equipment out!" Palmdale was miles away, but there was no other emergency field.

The dark outlines of trees loomed larger as the plane lost altitude. It was useless to lower the landing gear, because there was no place to land.

Swinging around in her seat, Mrs. Root said to Krumweide: "Don't worry about hanging from a tree, Dougie—California is using the gas chamber now."

Barely were the words out of her mouth than the motor started. The trees vanished. The dog relaxed. Krumweide, recalling the incident, said, "Mrs. Root met the challenge of death unafraid. There was no trace of panic. I've never seen such complacency."

When the plane put down, the dog jumped out, headed for a pan of water under a dripping spigot at the edge of the field, and drained it of every drop. Mrs. Root named him "Emergency," and the pilot took him home to his two daughters.

She was a freshman in college the day her father said to her, "Gladys, you ought to be on the stage—not the theater, but life's real stage: the courtroom."

"Would it please you very much, Daddy, if I became a lawyer?" she asked.

The smile lighting his face furnished the answer.

So to the courtroom dramas went Gladys Towles Root, actress, attorney, noncomformist, woman—a combination that punctures many a male ego, destroying the theory of man's superiority in the legal profession.

Her accomplishments consist, in addition to already listed skills, of a phenomenal memory, the ability to talk on the telephone, write a letter, and listen to three different conversations at the same time—plus a hard, cold, logical mind.

Many of her courtroom battles are strategically planned during the middle of the night while she has her feet massaged or her hair dyed.

Those who haven't seen her in action wonder if the costliness of her clothes and jewels would prejudice women jurors. The answer is an unequivocal *no*. Perhaps if her clothing were conventional, women on the juries would identify with her, becoming resentful. But the costumes worn by Mrs. Root are costumes jurors couldn't or wouldn't wear.

The bizarreness, the flamboyance, the ornateness are for one woman only: Gladys Root.

The first time Douglas Krumweide did her hair she told him, "Never get it too symmetrical. Sweep it here and gather it there and let it hang where it may. I never want it just perfect, or dormant like a wig. Make it appear alive. The more you whip it around and fool with it, the better I like it. I like angles."

The angles—district attorneys can attest, after hearing her cross-examinings—are not all confined to her hair.

6

THE "ROBOT MAN"

Mrs. Root's marriage to Frank Root lasted eleven years, ending with a divorce in 1941, at which time her son, Robert Towles Root, was eight years old. Two years later she wedded John C. Geiger. This marriage, punctuated with gaiety and sadness, continued until 1958, when Geiger died after a prolonged illness. The couple had one child, Christina, born in 1944.

Mrs. Root, who when, as customarily, was swathed in yards of clothing and tightly corseted could have concealed a miniature mountain without public detection, had no difficulty hiding her pregnancies. Less than two weeks before delivery of her children she was vigorously defending clients.

Her career had rocketed, sweeping her to both fame and widespread notoriety, professional and social. Opposing lawyers no longer took her lightly. In the courtroom she was feared and respected. More than thirty graduating law students had received training in her office. Now that the name of Root was firmly established, she decided, despite her new marriage, to retain it.

Few could have been better suited as a mate than Geiger, called Jay by his legion of friends. The West Coast repre-

sentative of a national fashion magazine, who later became
his wife's business manager, Geiger's fame as a grotesque
dresser equaled that of Mrs. Root. At a party the couple
hosted in Honolulu, Mrs. Root greeted her guests in a sheath-
like gown with multi-colored sequins, ending in a bouffant
swirl of shocking-pink ostrich plumes just below the knee.
Completing the ensemble was a lei of pink anthuriums.

At her side, Geiger was clad in a pink satin tuxedo. Favor-
ites of his wardrobe included coral-colored accordion-pleated
dinner jackets with matching satin shirts. For informal wear
while lolling around the house, he wore sequin shirts and
soft slacks having cummerbunds reaching almost to his arm-
pits.

Wherever Mr. and Mrs. Geiger went on the Islands, newspaper reporters and columnists pulled out note pads and
began scribbling. A column called "Chit Chat . . . On This
and That" kept abreast of her social schedule.

Cocktails are cocktails . . . whether they're served in lov-
ing cups or fruit jars . . . or so we thought until we heard
what Arthur Ostap, manager of the Surf Bar at the Royal
Hawaiian, has been up to this past week.

Cocktails for Mrs. John C. Geiger, well known LA attorney vacationing here now, are never served in the ordinary kind of glass. That just wouldn't fit in the picture at all.

Every time Mrs. Geiger appears in the dining room for
dinner dressed in another spectacular gown which her husband designs for her, it's no time at all before Arthur, himself, appears with a drink either the same color as the gown
or arranged in a setting which complements.

One night Mrs. Geiger featured vanda orchids in long leis
and in her hair. The drink that followed through in no time
was champagne with vandas floating in it and arranged in
ice around the base of the glass.

Last Sunday night Mrs. Geiger's costume was made of a
native print and set off with plumerias. Her creme de menthe

liqueur was served in a torch ginger flower which had been scooped out in the center. Around the base were red roses partially buried in shaved ice.

Mrs. Root, who does not like the taste of alcohol, out of deference to the manager's efforts sipped these drinks slowly.

Geiger, whenever asked about the extent of his wife's wardrobe, was uncertain, speculating that there were "more than seventy-five pairs of shoes, probably a hundred hats— all wide-brimmed—and then I lose count." Commenting on the furnishings of their home, he said, "We both like sequins, mirrors, velvet and satin, and you'll find evidence of this everywhere in the house."

His wife's extravagances, nonconformities and weird whims were not only willingly indulged but encouraged by him. The couple were frequently seen in nightclubs, dancing together, gliding to music with the rhythm and grace of professional entertainers. Though both were highly individualistic and extroverted, neither made efforts to take the spotlight of attention from the other.

It was while dining at the fashionable Tail of the Cock Restaurant in Beverly Hills one evening that Mrs. Root asked abruptly, "Do you smell gas, Jay?"

Her husband, leaning back in his chair so that the faint essence of garlic clinging to the ragout of lamb wouldn't affect his sense of smell, sniffed the air.

"All I can smell, honey, is 'Christmas Night,' " he said.

"It was only a figure of speech."

At first puzzled by the answer, Geiger suddenly seemed to understand. "Allan Adron?" he asked.

"Who else?"

She was referring to her latest client, whose knowledge of astrology should have forewarned him that the moon wasn't in a favorable position for him on that evening of October 26, 1949, when he shot and killed 32-year-old Jerome Ferreri.

Reaching across the table, Geiger patted her hand. "You'll do all right," he predicted.

Absently stirring a demi-tasse the waiter set before her, she replied, "I'll have to find some sort of a miracle to save this man."

"You won't find a miracle, you'll make one," her husband assured her.

Mrs. Root suggested, "Let's go home, Jay. I want to work on the color schemes for the week in court."

"Has Adron expressed his preference?"

"Yes," she said, explaining, "there's not much sameness. He's a strange man, of varying moods."

Mrs. Root has assiduouly studied colors and their psychological effects, and they have assumed vast importance to her practice. She knew that the correct colors can make a home comfortable, warm, friendly; the wrong colors, inhospitably cold, uninviting. In an office, poor choice of colors can destroy employee morale. In a restaurant color may encourage or diminish appetite. But chiefly, she has learned that colors can have a pronounced effect on a jailed person awaiting trial.

Upon taking a case one of her first questions is, "What's your favorite color?" Learning his or her choice, she wears this basic color around her client before and during trial, maintaining it to put the worried person at ease. This often has included her hair coloring, dyed daily to match her costumes.

Only once did Mrs. Root in her imitations of the spectrum run into difficulties. The incident was mentioned by Bill Kennedy, *Los Angeles Herald-Examiner* columnist. According to Kennedy she tried fluorescent dye and couldn't get rid of the stuff, so she used disinfectant, but that made her hair fall out.

Newspaper circulation boomed after the murder of Jerome Ferreri at his fifteen-room home, within walking distance of Gladys Root's dwelling. Mainly responsible for increased paper sales was Ferreri's wife, Betty, 26, curvaceous and red-haired—any court reporter's descriptive dream—who, according to preliminary hearings, confessed to hacking her husband twenty-seven times with a meat cleaver after he was first shot by Adron. Also involved was Charles Fauci, a friend of Mrs. Ferreri's, a small-time gangster believed to have furnished the murder weapon.

Three weeks after the killing, when the corpse of Ferreri—a man later to be described by Deputy District Attorney J. Miller Leavy as "tempestuous, obstreperous, ferocious, turbulent, quarrelsome and vicious"—was cooling in its grave, Allan Adron, restless, discouraged, the bright blood of anger burning on his cheeks, paced his cell like a jungle beast.

A friend had brought him a batch of newspapers. After reading about himself, his temper rocketed. It was then that he made a decision. He had heard of Gladys Root. He wanted her. He sent for her.

She came at once to visit him at the Los Angeles County Jail. While the jailer fitted the key to the lock she had an opportunity to study Adron. She saw a six-foot, 190-pound man with fair skin and straight brown hair. His walk was military. His eyes were a piercing hazel.

"Mrs. Root?" His voice was eager.

"Yes."

He came directly to the point. "I want you to be my lawyer."

She was mildly surprised. Although she had come to see Adron at his insistence, she knew he already had counsel. Furthermore, even though her knowledge of the case was superficial, it appeared that the position of Allan Adron was hopeless.

She reminded him, "You have representation—Mr. Jack Hardy."

Adron thrust his pale, anemic face close to hers. "I don't want Mr. Hardy," he said in a rising voice.

She asked why.

"Because I don't want to be thrown to the lions."

"What prompts you to say that?"

He went to his bed and picked up several newspapers. Waving them, he asked, "Have you been following the case?" She shook her head, replying, "Not closely. I've been too busy."

Thrusting the newspapers toward her, he said in an agitated voice, "Read for yourself what they've printed about me!"

"Suppose you tell me," she suggested.

"I will," Adron said, becoming calmer. "I may be a lot of things, Mrs. Root, but one thing I'm not is a fool. Most of these stories must have been given out by my attorney. I'm going to be railroaded. I'm going to be the fall guy. I know it."

"Mr. Adron," Mrs. Root asked softly, "just how did you reach this conclusion?"

Adron took a deep breath, expelling the air through his nose before replying. "I've advanced money for this case. Betty Ferreri talked me into it . . . to be used for her defense, Mr. Fauci's, and my own. Then I read in the papers that Betty had been more or less keeping me—that she felt sorry for me, because I was an insane man.

"Do you think I'm insane, Mrs. Root?" he asked pointedly.

"No, Mr. Adron, I do not."

He smiled. "Thank you, Mrs. Root," and continued: "I don't like Mr. Hardy. He said the only chance I had of getting off was to be sure Mrs. Ferreri got off first. If she didn't get off, nobody else was going to get off. Unless I subjugated my defense everybody would be found guilty, especially if she was found guilty. She had to get off. She had to come first."

The jailer approached. "Much longer, Mrs. Root?" he inquired.

"Just a few minutes," she told him, and turning back to the prisoner, asked. "What did you tell Mr. Hardy?"

Adron said, "I told him he was going to put her first and in order to do that, he worked me around so that I don't have any defense. I said, 'You plan to use me as Mrs. Ferreri's defense and I am not her defense and I'm not going to be.' "

He began striding back and forth as he said, "I can see the handwriting on the wall. They're going to cast doubts on my sanity . . . try to have me declared presently insane and probably condemned for life to a hospital for the . . . for the . . . what do you call it?"

"Criminally insane," she interjected.

"That's right. If this happens, my mouth will be sealed and the case against Mrs. Ferreri and Fauci will go up in smoke. And where will I be? Locked up forever."

Adron pulled out a handkerchief and wiped his damp forehead. He looked appealingly at Mrs. Root.

"May I ask you a personal question, Mr. Adron?"

He nodded permissively. "Ask anything you wish."

"Have you ever been in a hospital for the insane?"

"I have. A number of them."

"And were you discharged and pronounced cured?"

"I was. In Washington, D.C."

"Level with me, please, Mr. Adron," Mrs. Root said. "Did you kill Mr. Ferreri?"

"I did," Adron readily admitted, "but . . ."

Mrs. Root held up her hand protestingly. "I don't want your reasons or the circumstances. Not just yet."

Adron turned his eyes on her. The last sentence provided him with a wisp of hope.

"Does that mean, Mrs. Root, that you'll take my case?"

She hesitated before answering. "You're in a very awkward position, Mr. Adron. If I take your case, *I'll* be in an awkward position. I'll be accused of 'client snatching' and 'unethical practice' and Lord knows what else."

"But, Mrs. Root, you—you'll defend me, won't you?" he entreated in a weak voice.

"Of course, I will, Mr. Adron," she answered without hesitation.

For the first time in three weeks Allan Adron grinned broadly.

Her opening action was to send a note to Jack Hardy, copies of which went to the judge and the district attorney. Then she moved to set on the court calendar a motion to substitute counsel.

Attorney Hardy immediately dispatched a letter to Mrs. Root, alleging unethical practice and hinting that he would take her before the State Bar if she entered the case.

Mrs. Root did not scare easily; she energetically swung into the case. Three private investigators attached to her office dug deeply into the background of Adron. She learned that he was 52 years old, born in New England, reared by strict parents. He had little formal education. A very spiritual man, he loved reading and classical music and was fond of poetry. His passions were astrology and mythology, particularly the Greek gods.

Soft-spoken, Adron was careful of his choice of language and diction. He had a better-than-average political awareness and would attempt to figure out the moves of politicians in government. His interest in politics developed when he worked in Washington as valet to an ambassador.

Becoming ill, he was admitted to a Veterans' Hospital. Ultimately he became a mental case and was confined to several Federal hospitals, the last one in Washington, D.C., where he spent sixteen years before being released.

Then Adron came to California, where he performed odd jobs such as gardening and maintenance for private residences. He had good taste and spent his spare money on quality food and fashionable clothing. When he read a newspaper advertisement placed by Betty Ferreri for a handy-man or maintenance man, he checked the address and found it to be located in a rather exclusive and expensive district of Los Angeles. This appealed to him. He applied for the job.

Hired, he moved into the fifteen-room house, his duties consisting of answering the telephone, taking care of the Ferreri's eight-year-old boy, and keeping the house in general repair.

Attorney Jack Hardy rang the gong sounding the opening round of the legal battle with a motion that Adron be declared legally insane and his testimony, consequently, incompetent. The motion was protested by Mrs. Root. A sanity hearing was scheduled to be held before Superior Judge Charles W. Fricke.

When Mrs. Root asked what color Adron would like her to wear during the sanity hearing, his answer had been, "Blue with some bright red."

She obliged by appearing in a blue peau de soie suit. Her hat was thirty-seven inches wide, with an egg-shaped crown. The only breaking of the predominant blue was a big bouquet of red chiffon poppies under the brim of the hat. Her shoes and purse were blue and to her purse was fastened a huge red emblem of initials.

At the counsel table the heads of Mrs. Root and Adron at times moved close together as they whispered. Contrary to the beliefs of others, they were not talking about the case. They were speaking of Zeus, Apollo, Aphrodite and other gods and goddesses of Greek mythology.

It was a field day for doctors.

The first witness, Dr. Franklin H. Garrett, superintendent of the California State Mental Hospital at Norwalk, testified that he had examined Adron and found that the accused man was "not normal mentally and could not defend himself in a normal, straightforward manner."

While admitting that he found no evidence of delusions or hallucinations on the part of Adron, he said he was unable to decide whether statements made by him were all rational.

"Adron's ailment is dementia praecox," he said.

Another specialist, Dr. Frederick J. Hacker, operator of a psychiatric clinic in Beverly Hills, followed Dr. Garrett to the stand. He testified that he had examined Adron and found him to be suffering from schizophrenia.

Asked by Mrs. Root about Adron's ability to remember details of the slaying, Dr. Hacker replied, "A paranoic sometimes has phenomenal capacity to remember. They frequently have exceptional memories, these men with mental illnesses. They may have much better memories, shall I say, than you or I."

The third specialist to occupy the witness chair was Dr. Simon J. Conrad, psychiatrist for the California State Department of Mental Hygiene. He said he had come to the conclusion that Adron had been mentally ill continuously for three decades. He claimed that Adron was in a paranoic state but that his condition was not sufficiently deteriorated to be considered schizophrenia.

Judge Fricke entered into the discussion after Dr. Conrad stated that he did not consider it possible for a patient in a mental hospital to be cured and yet have his cure go undetected by doctors at the institution.

"Have you ever read Maudsley's *Criminal Responsibility of the Insane?*" Judge Fricke asked.

"No," Dr. Conrad answered.

"You might find it interesting," the judge commented.

There had been disagreement in the testimony of the specialists. It was now up to Judge Fricke to decide whether Allan Adron was sane or insane. The learned magistrate had made a study of criminal psychiatry for thirty years.

Judge Fricke made his decision. "Although the diagnoses of the specialists vary," he announced, "this court feels that Allan Adron is mentally capable of defending himself against the charges in this case."

A date was set for the trial without jury.

Mrs. Root rolled up her sleeves and pitched into the case, working far into the nights to build a defense. She ran smack into a barrier: Allan Adron. He seemed reluctant to confide in his counselor and his memory faltered when asked to go over his movements, step by step, the night of the shooting.

"Allan," she pleaded. "Try to remember. You've got to."

"I can't," he kept repeating.

Mrs. Root didn't believe his answer. She kept wondering, "What's blocking him mentally?" That night, unable to sleep, she quietly slipped from bed at 3 A.M., put on a robe, and went downstairs. She opened the lanai door and walked out into the balmy California night, pausing at the side of the swimming pool and staring into the placid waters. She saw the reflections of dozens of stars, until a slight breeze sprang up to ripple them away.

But just before this happened she snapped her fingers and cried into the darkness, "I think I've got it!"

The sight of the stars shimmering in the pool had triggered a hunch. Following it up, she telephoned the owner of a drug store where she traded. She had been fishing in troubled waters with Adron without getting a bite. It was time to change bait.

"Mr. Quint," she informed the sleepy voice answering the phone, "this is Gladys Root."

Roused from his warm bed, the druggist asked irritably what she wanted.

"A magazine from your store," she told him.

He gasped. "At this hour?"

"The hour doesn't matter, Mr. Quint."

"It does to me," he returned. "I'm a family man and this happens to be the middle of the night."

Mrs. Root said, "Far be it from me to separate you from your family, Mr. Quint. Just hand me the drug store key when I ring your doorbell. I'll return it in fifteen minutes. And," she added, "I'll make this favor up to you."

The druggist protested, but Mrs. Root overcame his arguments. Opening the store door, she located the light switch and went to the magazine rack. Here she saw six magazines dealing with the subject that interested her.

She chose one: *Horoscope*. She had seen a copy in Adron's cell.

The next day, hardly had she settled herself in Adron's cell than she asked, "Under what sign of the zodiac were you born, Allan?"

He perked up. "Why, I'm a Scorpio."

Her eyes searched the cell, coming to rest on a stack of magazines. Riffling through them, she held up a copy of *Horoscope*.

"Do you read this every day?"

"Yes," Adron replied. "It's got the Scorpio Daily Activity Guide. Tells me what to expect and advises me what to do from day to day."

"And do you follow it faithfully?"

"Oh, yes. Faithfully. I'm guided by it."

She rolled up the magazine in her hand and said, "Look, Allan. I'm going to take this with me and. . . ."

"No!" Adron cried loudly, ordering, "Don't take it! I'll need the advice from it tomorrow."

Adron had made a point: that he only read the predictions from day to day—none in advance. This was what she had hoped to discover.

"I'm taking this for only one reason," she explained. "So that you can have your personal daily horoscope prepared by an expert. This magazine has mass predictions. From now on you'll get individual predictions from [she mentioned a world-famous authority]. How would you like that, Allan?"

"I'd love it," he said, "but the expense. I can't afford. . . ."

"Hang the expense. It'll be my present to you."

Back in her office, Mrs. Root opened the magazine she had taken from Adron, turning the pages to his daily horoscope. Her intuitive flash had been correct. The periodical revealed that the past few days for the Scorpio-born had been "unfavorable for discussing any previous events in your life." Now she knew for certain why Adron had been noncommittal.

She sought the advice of the astrologer she had mentioned to Adron—a high-priced seer who had amassed a fortune by private appointments and readings to movie stars. From him she received a daily report covering the next seven days in the life of Adron.

After digesting the contents, she called one of her secretaries and dictated a rewrite of the predictions. Much of the original text was used, but here and there she made insertions, like the advice contained in the first two days: "Trust no one who is not a member of your immediate family," and "Do not discuss your personal problems with anyone."

If Adron by any chance suspected rigged charts, the fact that these first two reports followed the trend of advice offered by his magazine should allay his suspicions.

For the remaining five days she wrote unsubtle hints that she hoped would loosen his lips, such as "Any aid given to another person who is trying to help you will be well rewarded and may even save your life."

As was expected, Adron was uncooperative the first two days after she handed him the charts. He would read them carefully before their talks. Mrs. Root patiently sat through two meetings which gained her nothing. On the third day, the moment he finished reading he appeared a changed person. His eyes sparkled. Words fairly tumbled from his lips.

"Ask me any questions and I'll answer them," he promised. She requested a detailed account of the night of the slaying. Adron wasted no time. "Betty," he said, "told me and Fauci that her husband would get a cat or a dog and bring it home for a pet and then in front of her little boy he would tease the pet and slowly kill it. Then he would take the pet and hang it on a line and make the child do a war dance around the dead animal, until she would become hysterical.

"She said he would be cruel to her during sex acts and tell her of his conduct with other women. And she said that I was going to be her savior—that I was a fine man with a fine understanding.

"She said to me, 'Allan, if somebody was going to kill you, what would you do?' 'I said if I knew somebody was going to kill me, I'd kill the sonofabitch first.' 'Well,' she said, 'Jerry is going to come back and kill me.'

" 'Allan, you've got to help me.'

"I told her that I was disabled, had an ulcer and was no match physically for Ferreri. But she insisted over and over again that I had to help her. She said that Fauci had a gun— that she'd get Jerry into the butler's pantry and that I should take the gun to my room. And when I heard her scream, I was to come out and help her.

"Later that evening I heard a scratching sound at my window. I raised it and saw Fauci there with a gun. He said, 'Don't you hear her screaming? She needs your help. Here, take this gun and help her.'

"I took the gun and went toward the kitchen. The lights were out. I heard Mrs. Ferreri calling for help. I saw Jerry dimly. I started shooting. I fired three times and then the gun jammed. I pulled so hard I thought the trigger would break.

"The lights went on and I saw Jerry sprawled on the floor. He rose up. I moved into the butler's pantry and grabbed him by the neck. I beat him on the back of the head and neck with the gun.

"Betty said, 'Don't let him up, Allan. I'm going to help you. I've got a cleaver.'

"She commenced beating him over the left side of the head with the cleaver. I gave him a couple of more whacks with the gun barrel. I suddenly got tired and stopped. The gun was stuck on my finger. Fauci appeared with a towel on his hand. He wiggled the gun off my finger. I went to my room but I could still hear Betty whacking at her husband . . . heard the meat cleaver hitting his skull."

Adron was perspiring freely when he finished, his eyes wild.

"Are you sure you'll remember this story, Allan?" Mrs. Root asked.

"I'll try," he said, "If you'll wear a certain kind of dress to please me."

"You name it," she encouraged. "I'll wear anything you want but tights."

He chuckled and then grew silent, thinking. At length he said, "I've got it. You wear a metallic silver dress and my favorite flower, a beautiful red rose."

There was no time to call her modiste, so she shopped until she found a dress that might appeal to him. It was silver lamé. She decided to wear a cross of amethyst and diamonds—a pin four inches long. She knew Adron, being a highly spiritual man, would approve.

Her mind playing with ideas for Adron's defense, she visited the scene of the murder, roamed around the house. One object in particular held her attention. How important it was, she had to be sure. She thought there was a way to assay its value to the case. She visited her client again, carrying with her a loudly ticking Big Ben alarm clock she had purchased on the way to the jail. She set it on the cement floor between them. Adron lifted his eyebrows quizzically in the direction of the clock, but asked no questions.

They conversed. The Big Ben ticked away with metronome regularity.

Adron was talking, staring at the cell wall. The words came easily. His memory seemed fresh. Suddenly Mrs. Root interrupted him by shouting: "Allan, kill him! . . . kill him! . . . kill him!"

Adron jumped to his feet. His eyes blazed. With his arm extended toward the wall, his forefinger moved back and forth in a manner simulating the squeezing of a trigger. So vivid was his pantomiming that Mrs. Root could easily imagine a gun clutched in his hand.

"That's enough, Allan," her voice commanded.

Adron sprawled into his chair, near the point of collapse. The fire in his eyes died. They became vacant and then normal.

"What happened?" he gasped.

"Something very good, Allan," she said cheerfully. "I'll see you tomorrow."

That night as she lay in bed scribbling notes in red ink, which she would later review and commit to memory, she turned toward her husband.

"You know, Jay, I can't smell the gas anymore."

He laid aside the book he was reading. Interpreting her thoughts, he said, "You've created the miracle then?"

She laughed. "Miracle or mirage, I don't know which . . . yet."

Jay Geiger didn't offer the cliché of "Get some sleep." He knew it was futile. He also knew that a scant few hours' sleep would sharpen and oil rather than corrode her steel-trap mind. He knew that when she finally placed the notebook on the end table and turned out the lights, there would be no further need for it. Whatever she had scribbled would be etched unforgettably on her mind.

If the press had been groping for a nickname to christen Allan Adron, the search was ended the initial day of the trial.

Mrs. Root based her defensive maneuvers on a theory that Adron was insane and under "hypnotic suggestion" at the time of the killing, but was now perfectly sane.

The press dubbed him the "Robot Man."

Mrs. Root attempted to prove that Betty Ferreri had aroused a feeling of sympathy and used her womanly wiles, augmented by the power of suggestion and coupled with Adron's affection for the little Ferreri boy, to control his mind.

"I will prove that he had been set up, prepared, and conditioned for days," she told the court.

As the trial began, Mrs. Root observed that Mrs. Ferreri was seated in a position facing Adron. Her eyes seemed to be glowering at him. Fearful of any influence she might exercise upon him, Mrs. Root took care of this situation by leaning forward, the immensity of her hat blocking off sight of Mrs. Ferreri.

The opening testimony, given by Dr. K. Grosvenor Bailey, favored her client. Dr. Bailey stated: "For three months Adron had lived in the Ferreri home in a highly disturbing atmosphere that could have driven even a sane person crazy. In my opinion, he was conditioned by an evening of coaching, appealed to by Mrs. Ferreri, aided by Fauci."

Dr. Bailey added that "this was when the 'robot complex' took command. He was an automaton pure and simple."

Mrs. Root had only one question to ask Dr. Bailey: "Do you consider Allan Adron sane now?"

"Yes," Dr. Bailey answered.

Another witness aiding Mrs. Root was Dr. Victor Parkin, who pointed out that the accused had been in and out of institutions for twenty years since he had suffered a mental breakdown following World War I service.

He was asked the same question by Mrs. Root that she had asked Dr. Bailey: "Do you consider Allan Adron sane now?"

"I do," Dr. Parkin replied.

As the trial approached the final day, Mrs. Root paid another visit to Adron in his cell and told him she was going to place him on the witness stand.

They discussed clothing and Adron made his choice. It was white.

For one of the most important days of the trial she appeared in a white woolen suit. It had gold stars on a sailor collar, lending an overall military effect. She added these touches because in her talks with the defendant he made frequent mention of the armed forces. Her skirt was pleated. White shoes and gold jewelry completed her costume.

Adron's eyes sparkled. "Wonderful," he complimented.

Mrs. Root felt that she had to set the stage for Adron. The experiment in his cell with the alarm clock had proved to her beyond any doubt that he was a schizophrenic, highly susceptible to sound, and that anything repetitious such as the loud ticking of a clock could control his mind. Adron, she firmly believed, had to be practically under the influence of hypnosis in order to remember details and fully react to the questions she planned to ask him.

Simultaneously with putting Adron on the stand, she had a grandfather clock carried into the courtroom—the same one that she had seen on her visit to the Ferreri household. She was of the opinion that the clock had played an important role in disciplining his mind the night of the slaying.

The clock was introduced as evidence over the objections of the prosecutor.

Adron took the stand. Near him, the clock ticked away and the pendulum swung back and forth. The sound and the pendulum fascinated him. They refreshed his mind, guided him, as the Big Ben had done.

Mrs. Root said, "As you left your room to help Mrs. Ferreri, what did the ticking of this clock seem to say to you?"

"It kept repeating, COME . . . COME . . . COME," Adron answered.

"And what did Mrs. Ferreri say?"

"She said, 'Allan, SHOOT! . . . SHOOT! . . . SHOOT!'."

In her summation Mrs. Root stated that nothing could be left to Adron's judgment. His mind had to be held . . . a brake fastened on it. Then it could be controlled.

"The clock," she said, "was the brake and both the ticking and swinging of the pendulum combined to induce a hypnotic state. Betty Ferreri's commands of SHOOT! . . . SHOOT! . . . SHOOT! were synchronized with the TICK . . . TICK . . . TICK of the clock.

"At this particular time Allan Adron had no conception of right or wrong."

Judge Fricke came in immediately with his decision.

Allan Adron was freed of the murder charge.

A smile spread over the face of the "Robot Man." He turned toward his attorney. She reached out her hand and firmly pinned his against the surface of the counsel table. The pressure implied restraint. One of Mrs. Root's pet aversions was for any of her clients, overcome with joy, to embrace her.

During the trial that followed—of Betty Ferreri and Charles Fauci—without Mrs. Root to control him, Adron proved a belligerent witness, frequently engaging in word battles and hot temper flare-ups against attorney Jack Hardy. However, the fact remained that Jerome Ferreri, while he might have continued to live for "half an hour" after Adron shot him, would have died whether or not his wife hacked his skull with a meat cleaver.

No complicity could be attached to Fauci.

The jury returned a verdict of not guilty for both defendants.

Early in the Adron case, Mrs. Root had experienced severe stomach twinges. She blamed them on a craving for chocolates. Her diagnosis was incorrect. Her appendix ruptured.

Upon reading that she was hospitalized, Adron called, bringing her gifts of fancy canned imports. A year later he wrote her a lengthy letter postmarked from the East Coast. The contents spoke mostly of the clothes worn during the trial, and he wondered if she were still wearing them.

Had he been better acquainted with Mrs. Root's habits, he would have known that on the day following his acquittal the wardrobe worn during the trial had been bestowed upon her grateful maids.

7

POTPOURRI

Reaching into the brown paper bag, the Skid Row bum unscrewed the cap from a bottle of Muscatel and with a backward flip of his hand sailed it down the alley. There was no need to recap the bottle. The bum and his two expectant companions lounging against the back of a building would see to that.

The owner of the Muscatel, allowing only the neck of the bottle to protrude from the bag—standard drinking procedure for this section of the city—raised it to his lips. Then, changing his mind, he lowered the bottle a few inches.

"Come on, Jack, drink up," one of his friends pleaded.

Jack shook his head. Known as "The Bard of Main Street," he was aware that this was one time he had a captive audience. He intended to make the most of it.

"First a toast," he proposed.

His impatient friends waited, thirst written upon their faces, for the doggerel they knew would gush forth. They prayed it would be short.

The bum, his wine-sodden thought correlated, raised the bottle:

"Root-de-toot, root-de-toot,
Here's to Gladys Towles Root.
Her dresses are purple, hats wide,
She'll get you one instead of five."

Less than two blocks from this convivial scene, on the site
of the departed and legendary Rainbow Saloon at 212 South
Hill Street, stood the new and resplendent office of Gladys
Root. The Rainbow, a monument to drabness before its
demise, had blended into its environment without a struggle.

This segment of Los Angeles, although it touched the
spanking newness of the Civic Center, was run down. There
were ptomaine-type restaurants, parking lots, and old frame
hotels whose longevity depended upon the course of a care-
lessly thrown cigarette.

The heads of the pedestrians who walked this area were
not stuffed with grandiose schemes. For the most part they
carried only broken, twisted dreams. Much could be fore-
told by watching their feet. They shuffled along aimlessly
and one prophecy was undeniable: they were not pointed in
the direction of success.

Illuminating the dinginess with the brightness of a Klieg
light—and as one startled observer described it: "Like a new
suit worn over dirty underwear"—the office of Gladys Root
flashed with the brilliance of the Hope diamond.

The façade is black stone trimmed in gold, but elsewhere
on the outside and inside of the building her notorious passion for purple asserts itself. The door is purple glass. Her
name on the window is purple script trimmed in gold. Inside the door one's feet sink into soft purple carpeting. Rugs,
furnishings, and drapes are all the same eye-popping purple;
the flower pots, containing artificial orchids, are of course
purple. There are fourteen rooms, including a law library
done in sea-green, a black marble bathroom containing a
contour tub built to fit the bodily dimensions of Mrs. Root, a
spacious dining room and kitchen.

Coincidental though it was, the office was appropriately located directly across the street from the Los Angeles City
Fire Department Headquarters. There was a strong similarity
between the two establishments: they rivaled each other in
speed. In answer to a call the fire trucks roared into Hill
Street, racing to extinguish flames somewhere in the vast city.
Mrs. Root, in answer to a call from a jailed client, bounded
hell-bent from her glass-fronted door to administer aid, comfort, and counsel to someone who had run afoul of the law.

The door, which withstood the rapid entrances and exits
of Mrs. Root, was, five weeks after installation, shattered by
the body of a drunk after a forcible ejection from the office.
The drunk, wandering from his Skid Row stamping grounds,
had lurched into the law offices believing them to be the
Rainbow Saloon.

The metamorphosis overwhelmed him. Those in alcoholic
stupors are alleged to see pink, as in elephants. This veteran
imbiber of the grape saw purple, as in Root. Sudden sight of
the unexpected caused him to go berserk. It required the
combined efforts of the office staff males to bounce him into
the street. Here, his dignity destroyed and, he thought, deprived of his rights as a citizen, he pirouetted, came charging
back crying, "I want a drink!" and his shoulder shattered the
glass door. The mishap had a sobering effect. Quickly he
surveyed the wreckage, panicked, and fled.

The next day, exuding only a trace of alcoholic fumes, he
returned to the scene of destruction, demanding to see "the
head of the business," and as Mrs. Root's secretary informed
her, threatening to sue.

"Shall I call the police?" the secretary asked.

"Show him in," Mrs. Root said, putting aside some important trial papers. "His nerve appeals to me."

Entering the office, the visitor took one glance at her and
gasped, "My God! You're Gladys Root!" He clutched at the
desk for support.

"And you are? . . . ."

"A knucklehead," he sputtered and shaking his head, muttered, "and to think I wanted to sue *you*."

"You have the right if you think you're justified in doing so," she told him.

"No, no," he said hurriedly, starting for the door. "I just wanta get outta here."

"Wait a second," she called.

He froze in his tracks.

"When did you eat last?"

"Eat," he repeated dumbly, as if he didn't understand the meaning of the word.

"Never mind," Mrs. Root said. "I was about to have lunch. Will you join me?"

He looked at his shoddy clothing and then at her indescribable apparel.

"I have a dining room here in the office," she explained.

He nodded.

Luncheon for two consisted of Caesar salad, filets of pompano Moscovite, and, for dessert, pears stuffed with marzipan and topped with strawberries.

His appetite was ravenous.

Before he parted company with Mrs. Root, he said, "I've been thinkin' I oughta pay for what I done to your door."

"Forget it," she advised.

He insisted, "No, I mean it."

She asked if he had any money and he told her not at present. She dipped into her purse and handed him a five-dollar bill.

"Let's pretend you sued me and collected these damages."

The grateful man, who left clutching the bill in his hand, was only a mild disturber of the peace compared with George Carlson, a demented individual now incarcerated in a mental institution. Carlson, freed by bail on a robbery charge, slipped unnoticed past the reception desk and made his way toward Mrs. Root's private office. He was convinced that the lawyer had supplied the police with information leading to his arrest.

He was going to kill her.

Opening the office door, he pulled out a gun, leveling it at her head. Inwardly Mrs. Root was trembling, but her voice was unemotional and a half-smile lit her face as she greeted, "Good afternoon, Mr. Carlson. What can I do for you?"

The answer came slowly. "It's not what you can do for me, it's what I'm going to do to you."

"What is that?" she inquired pleasantly.

"Pull this trigger," he said, waving the gun from side to side.

She thought rapidly. Her husband was in the next office and could perhaps hear her if she raised her voice. She had to stall for time and all the while slowly increase her voice volume, hopeful it would carry into the adjoining room.

"If you are going to kill me, Mr. Carlson," she began, "and your mind is made up, there is nothing I can do to stop you." Then she said louder, "But if you kill me with that gun you are pointing at me, why, the police are going to arrest you and you'll lose your own life."

She paused for breath and then, stepping up the volume to a frequency close to a shout, boomed, "KILLING ME WITH THAT GUN YOU HAVE IN YOUR HAND WON'T HELP MATTERS. IT'S EASY TO KILL. BUT STOP AND CONSIDER THE CONSEQUENCES. I. . . ."

Behind Carlson, the door burst open and Jay Geiger crisply ordered: "Put that gun down!"

Taken by surprise, Carlson obeyed. Geiger grabbed the gun and his wife telephoned the police.

In East Los Angeles, Mrs. Root was to face another gun. She had been retained to defend Ivan Peteroff, who shot and injured his factory boss. Peteroff was a resident of the Russian settlement. Deciding to do some of the spadework herself, Mrs. Root had her chauffeur drive her to the colony, bent on a personal investigation.

She was unprepared for the sight that greeted her at the address she had been given. It was the high holidays and the Russians, the men mostly bearded, were wearing hats and burning religious candles. They were mumbling prayers. The Russians weren't the only ones wearing hats. Mrs. Root had on one of her snappiest creations. A man approached her and she told him she was there on the Peteroff matter. He spoke a few unintelligible words, and within a matter of seconds another man appeared, pointing a rifle at her.

As Mrs. Root learned the next day, it was not known to members of the colony that she had been engaged to represent Peteroff, and they were convinced she had appeared to dig up evidence against him.

The Russian advanced toward her. She was squarely in the center of the rifle sight. His face was expressionless behind the covering of long whiskers.

Mrs. Root backed away, shouting, "Look! I'm your friend! I came here to help the boy, not to harm him!"

Her appeal failed to halt the Russian's movement. Whether or not he understood English she didn't know, but there was no time to find a translator. She fled, ran through the darkness to the car, hopped in and ordered the chauffeur, "Get the hell away from here—fast!"

The car took off. Shots echoed through the street.

"Swerve, swerve," Mrs. Root cried, sprawling on the floor.

A mile away the chauffeur stopped the car, alighting to survey the results of the gunfire.

"Only a little paint chipped off," he reported.

Mrs. Root commented, "How are they going to hit the moon if they can't hit a Cadillac?"

"I don't know, but they didn't do us any damage."

"Well, I wouldn't say that," Mrs. Root disagreed. "See what happened to my hat."

She held up her hat, a Spanish sailor straw covered with yellow feathers. It was irreparably crushed.

Mrs. Root, who has a love for Cadillacs, once defended a client with a burning affinity for the same make of car. Should he chance to see a new, shiny, glossy one, he pursued it and at the first opportunity—and there generally seemed to be an opportunity—stole it. No other car would do. It had to be a Cadillac.

Apprehended by the police—caught redhanded at the wheel of his latest illegal acquisition—he engaged Mrs. Root as counsel. She plotted a unique defense. It was an overpowering compulsion, an irresistible impulse causing the irrational action, that impelled him to steal, not just any kind of a car, but only the finest. There was a subconscious coercion in the act similar to that of an alcoholic craving a drink or a gambler risking everything at the gaming table.

He did not steal for profit, she pointed out. He stole only so he could attain an equal footing with the rich. She had the jury believing that General Motors should be indicted for manufacturing such a beautiful temptation. Labeling him a "harmless car kleptomanic," she postulated that when he slid into the driver's seat he became a different man, completely forgetting his troubles by reason of the tremendous lift it gave him.

"During these ecstatic moments," she said, "my client was a changed personality, deluding himself into believing he had reached the very pinnacle of success."

James Aguirre was acquitted.

Six months later, her husband drove her to a Hollywood restaurant. They were just finishing their dinner when she received a telephone call. It was from James Aguirre.

"I've done it again," he related. "I need you."

Returning to the table, she told her husband she would take a taxi to the jail. He said he would drive the car home and meet her later. At the jail she talked with Aguirre about his latest impulse. He freely confessed his guilt, and pleaded with her to try for another acquittal.

"When did the police pick you up?" she asked.

Before Aguirre could answer, the jailer appeared, to tell Mrs. Root she had a telephone call. Her husband was on the other end of the line.

"Gladys," he said, "the police called. Our car was stolen. I went home in a taxi. They caught the thief."

"What was his name?"

"James Aguirre."

"What!" she exclaimed.

"Do you happen to know him?"

She chuckled. "I'll tell you all about it when I get home."

Mrs. Root went back to the cell and told Aguirre she would be unable to handle his case.

"Why not?" he asked crestfallen.

"For a very valid reason."

"What is it?"

"Because in this case," she stated, "I'm the plaintiff. Out of thousands of Cadillacs in Los Angeles County, why, Mr. Aguirre, please tell me why, did you have to steal mine?"

Aguirre rubbed his chin, mulled the situation over, and replied, "Compulsion, I guess. Isn't that the word you used at my trial?"

Mrs. Root couldn't help laughing, "I'm not going to press charges against you," she said, "but I advise you to take your talents to another city."

Anything connected with animals, the weather, or Mrs. Root is the type of story that makes Los Angeles newspaper city desk men jump for joy. And when two of these elements

—Mrs. Root and a black cat—are interwoven, it's a double guarantee that linotype machines will start humming.

Clifton Buma, a dairy employee, hit a black cat with his car. He didn't have to stop, but being an animal lover he did. Getting out of his car, he chased the cat to learn how badly it had been hurt. As a result, he was shot in the shoulder and then arrested on suspicion of attempted burglary.

The case went before Municipal Judge Joseph Marchetti for a preliminary hearing.

John M. Young testified, under questioning by Deputy District Attorney Terrys Gambord, that he had heard a man walking in his driveway and had fired two shots. Then the man ran.

"Yes, I heard the shooting, but I didn't know what happened before," added Leona Neuman, Young's niece, a student at the University of Southern California.

"Maybe so," argued Gladys Root, defense counsel, "but everything proves that Buma was scared and immediately drove to a filling station, asking the attendant to call police and an ambulance."

"I've always told him black cats were unlucky," declared the defendant's wife, Betty, outside the courtroom. "Now he'll believe me."

Buma won a dismissal.

For those who imagine the pleasanter aspects of a lawyer's life include frequent trips to the bank to deposit huge fees, Mrs. Root will cite the case of an alleged rubber check artist she represented. His name was John Michelson and he was out on bail. His father, an upstanding citizen with a love for his wayward offspring, told Mrs. Root he would send his personal paycheck in with his son to pay the legal fees.

Michelson brought in three of his father's checks; Mrs. Root cashed them, extracted the fees, and gave the son the balance at his father's request. The day before trial he handed her his father's check for $1,800.

"Isn't this a little large?" she wondered.

He admitted it was much larger than the others, but he declared that it included a bonus and reminded her that the others had been good and there was no danger in endorsing it. This she did, taking a small amount for her work and handing the remainder to Michelson.

The trial was a one-day affair and Michelson went free. Soon afterwards, the bank called her. The check was a forgery. Michelson had copied his father's signature.

Mrs. Root wrote off $1,800 to experience.

Guns were not the only weapons faced by Mrs. Root. Once there was a knife: a long, curved, sharp butcher knife held in the hand of a Norwegian cook in the Geiger household. The lawyer's back was exposed and vulnerable to the knife, standing as she was by the stove preparing bouillabaisse. The cook had tried to make the soup the week before, but it was too thin and tasteless, so Mrs. Root was now giving her a culinary lesson.

Resentment had built up to the eruption level in the cook, who had been recently hired. It was during the war years and cooks were difficult to come by—and for any available, few references were required. Many of them were earning double their usual wages on defense-plant assembly lines. It would have been better for the welfare of Mrs. Root if that had been where this particular cook was employed instead of creeping up on her clutching a murderous knife.

"You must add some thyme and marjoram . . ." Mrs. Root began—then broke off suddenly as something seemed to warn her of the danger behind. She straightened up, wheeling around. The cook and knife were three feet away. Mrs. Root, aided by her four-and-a-half-inch spike heels, drew herself to her full height.

"Drop that knife!" she ordered.

The knife clattered on the linoleum floor, and the cook raced to the servants' quarters, where she locked herself in her room for twenty-four hours.

Mrs. Root and her husband consulted.

"I think I know how to smoke her out," she said.

"With smoke?"

"No. With soup. Same effect, I hope."

She prepared more bouillabaisse and, when it reached the simmering stage, set a potful down before the door of the servant's room. Using a magazine, she fanned the succulent odors so that they seeped under the door to reach the hungry domestic.

Then she waited patiently.

Fifteen minutes of torture was all the cook could take. The door opened cautiously and her head poked out. She looked famished.

"It's all yours, Helga," Mrs. Root said, indicating the pot of soup. "Eat up."

The cook spooned it into her mouth. Finished, she faced her employer.

"How was it, Helga?" Mrs. Root questioned.

The cook licked her lips to catch a final clinging drop and said, "I have to admit, ma'am, that it's very good."

"Would you say it's better the way I make it?"

Hanging her head in defeat, the cook admitted, "Yes, Mrs. Root."

Mrs. Root suggested she seek future employment at a defense plant.

One of Mrs. Root's favorite topics is rape. She contends: "There are three major types of rape: the invited, the brutal attack, and the under-age copulation. The brutal assault occurs perhaps once in ten thousand. Here the woman has to be knocked unconscious or forcibly seduced, perhaps by a gang, and spread-eagled. The attacks usually occur late at night and are generally perpetrated by groups of boys ranging in years from seventeen to their mid-twenties who prowl the streets in cars. When they spot an intended victim they force her into their car at the point of a knife or a gun.

"It's a very nasty business.

"The under-age type is fairly common. Here, the girl may willingly subject herself to intercourse, but the fact remains she's under eighteen, and often her parents or the district attorney press charges.

"The invited rape begins with the fashion designers who started the style for capris, bikinis, and tight slacks. In a manner of speaking, they are answerable to the charge, indirect as it may be. Into these articles of clothing that either expose or accentuate the bodily curves and bulges, steps a woman who has forgotten she is a lady. 'Lady' is a common word tossed about in everyday usage, but the literal meaning has been destroyed by bad conduct.

"Its meaning has been neglected in her appearance, her manners, her way of speaking, the places she goes and people she goes with. Her code of propriety, if she had one, has been discarded. Watch her, observe her actions and it will be immediately apparent whether or not there is a possibility she may some day be molested, raped, assaulted, even kidnapped.

"The average assault-with-intent-to-rape case consists of the following simple ingredients: a cocktail bar, and a woman who shouldn't be present without a proper escort. The second she walks through the door and becomes the cynosure of masculine eyes, she exposes herself to conditions that may lead to trouble.

"Women should not enter bars, even with a girl friend. A girl friend is no protection. If a woman is lonesome, there are other diversions. She can affiliate with an organization, a church, a social club. If she is a spiritually, educationally, physically and mentally well-adjusted woman, she will have no time to waste in drinking places.

"In the majority of the rape cases I've handled, the woman encouraged the man, gave willing consent, or invented the story."

Nearly a decade ago Mrs. Root was instrumental in breaking up a gang of teenagers—both boys and girls—engaged in a shakedown racket. They were students of a well-regarded high school in Los Angeles. For more than a year they operated undetected.

A girl would stand at a traffic light on a street leading to her school. As the light turned red and cars stopped, she would select one in which a lone man rode.

Then she would accost him with, "Mister, I wonder if you could give me a lift to my high school. I've missed the bus and I'm afraid I'll be late."

The driver was usually willing to oblige her. Within a few blocks, he was to discover he had made a serious mistake as he heard her say, "Now, Mister, listen to me carefully. Unless you give me ten dollars, I'm going to tear my dress and stockings and scream that you attacked me."

While the startled driver was trying to piece things together in his befuddled brain, the girl would press home her selling points. "You'll go to jail on a charge of molesting a teenager. You'll lose your job. And your wife, if you have one. You'll have a police record and be disgraced."

Untold hundreds of victims of this racket paid off. The boys worked an identical game on male drivers, claiming they would swear an attempt was made to molest them.

Mrs. Root defended a number of these car drivers who were guilty of nothing more than what they originally thought was an act of kindness in giving a boy or girl a lift to school. She lost several cases until one of the accused who refused to be taken told her he was incapable of the sex act.

A qualified doctor's examination substantiated the statement. It was then that Mrs. Root enlisted the aid of the police, who broke up the youthful gang.

Every morals case client of Mrs. Root is given a psychiatric examination to determine the extent to which his crime may have arisen from mental illness. If necessary and feasible, her office arranges for long-term therapy. She argues that perverts should not be sent to prisons, but to hospitals; that prisons often release them in a more dangerous condition than when they entered.

Mrs. Root once clashed with an austere Pasadena judge over the matter of castration, and her spate of angry, defiant words earned her a fine for contempt of court. He was a fervent believer in castration as a panacea for those convicted of morals offenses.

She described him privately as "a man sitting up and acting like he was God on the taxpayers' money."

To those appearing before him who were convicted of any form of sexual perversion, he would explain before passing sentence that there was one way to escape prison: castration. All they had to do was volunteer.

Those convicted, of course, didn't relish doing time. Many agreed, submitting to the judge's offer. They were promptly dispatched, along with a bailiff, to a doctor. The bailiff would witness and bring back signed proof that the doctor had performed the operation.

Mrs. Root had a case come before this judge. Her client was a young man of nineteen who had twice before been up on a charge of molesting boys of fourteen and fifteen. The boys had all been willing participants, as was the present alleged victim.

She insisted that the defendant see her psychiatrist. When he seemed unwilling, she said, "Look, if you have an illness, you go to a doctor and he can cure you. If you commit acts

of perversion, that also means you're sick. You go to a psychiatrist. There is a chance that he also can cure you. It's as
simple as that."

The youth consented, and Mrs. Root received a report
from the psychatrist that he had traced the beginning of the
boy's homosexuality to advances forced upon him by one of
the teachers at a military school.

"Can he be cured?" Mrs. Root inquired.

"A very good chance exists," the psychiatrist replied.

Mrs. Root lost the case and the judge made his usual propo-
sition to the defendant: castration or prison. A violent argument developed. Mrs. Root secured a writ restraining the
judge from future public advocacy of castration.

On prostitution and abortion, Mrs. Root has deep convictions and refuses to yield an inch in her thinking. "Prostitution," she says, "is going to be with us forever and a day.
The highest officials in the world have tried in vain to eliminate the oldest profession. It couldn't be done. Prostitutes
swarm over every country thick as a cloud of locusts. No
fewer than twenty thousand have always roamed the streets
and lolled in the restaurants and bars of Paris.

"It is fatuous to believe anything can be done about it. It is
a time-honored evil. You can close the brothels, but you
can't stop the women from walking the streets, or the new
mechanized pickup prostitution, where lone women or pairs
cruise in cars, seeking business. In Denmark they drive the
streets in small bed-equipped trucks, blowing their horns or
flashing lights to attract male attention.

"I am in favor of legalizing prostitution under stringent
laws that include inspection and medical supervision.

"The periodic police roundup of prostitutes is a sham that
wastes valuable police manpower and deludes the public into
thinking that vice is really being curbed."

Her opinion is that legalized abortion is, in the future, inevitable. "It comes under the heading of 'progress' and can't be stopped. The burgeoning population will raise a stentorian hue and cry to hold down the explosion, and abortion will take up the slack wherever birth control fails to do so.

"When the time is propitious, religious and other barriers will be hurdled and abortion will raise a lawful head. Then, not only will unemployment be held in check, but many a young woman could be saved whose life now may be ruined by a few minutes of reckless passion."

One of the wackiest cases Mrs. Root was ever connected with concerned a gardener accused of raping a maid who worked in a Beverly Hills mansion. The alleged action took place in the servants' quarters over the garage.

Mrs. Root took her client to a photographer for a series of close-up facial photos. She didn't believe that a physically husky woman like the maid could have been raped without putting up a strenuous fight, or that her teeth and fingernails would not have left telltale wounds. The face of the gardener was unmarked.

The maid testified that she was an invalid unable to run on account of an artificial leg; that she had a glass eye; that her hearing was faulty. And in this helpless state, she alleged, the gardener forced his attentions upon her.

"Did you fight against him?" Mrs. Root asked.

"Oh, yes, I certainly did," the maid replied. "I kept biting him in the face."

Photos were introduced showing the unscarred defendant. The prosecutor contended a photograph could be retouched, which threw some doubt on the credibility of the pictures.

During the trial Mrs. Root studied the maid, noting that when the gardener took the stand she displayed no animosity, but, on the contrary, reveled in his account of her being a willing partner in the act of copulation. She squirmed in her chair, her eyes became cloudy, her breathing heavy.

She's excited, reliving a pleasant experience, thought Mrs. Root.

A check of the medical history of the maid confirmed that she had a wooden leg and a glass eye, and a dental report showed false teeth—both uppers and lowers. Jury sympathy was inevitably going to gravitate toward a woman with these physical shortcomings unless Mrs. Root managed to nail her in her present dreamy state with one quick supposition before the prosecutor could voice objections.

Her client had related to her that he remembered the maid unscrewing her wooden leg to make herself more comfortable and taking out her false eye—but that was all.

During cross-examination, Mrs. Root delineated her version of the alleged seduction. Her voice was low and sexy. The maid closed her eyes, breathed raspingly, and the lawyer knew she was getting a vicarious thrill.

Mrs. Root picked up a paper sack from the counsel table and carried it to within a few feet of the plaintiff. Suddenly she pulled forth a standard water tumbler and spoke rapidly:

"Before having intercourse you took out your teeth and dropped them into a glass such as this one, didn't you?"

"Oh, yes, yes," the maid babbled. "I get excited and I didn't want to bite him."

The case against her client vanished.

Mrs. Root once won an embarrassing victory that is still talked about around the courthouse. It involved an alleged child molester. The case hinged upon the testimony of a ten-year-old child who went into detail as to how the accused, who had fondled her, first reached under her dress, examined the tiny pearl buttons on her panties, and was careful not to rip them or tear the button holes when he removed the garment.

When it came time for the defendant to testify, Mrs. Root, taking his arm, led him to the witness chair. He carried a white cane, denoting blindness, and stumbled pitifully trying to locate the stand. After he testified, Mrs. Root helped him back to the counsel table. The judge immediately dismissed the charges. No blind man could possibly have been so meticulous in his advances as the child claimed.

The defendant rose, facing the magistrate.

"Your Honor," he said, bowing, "thank you. The moment I came into this courtroom and looked at you, I knew you had an honest face."

Mrs. Root flushed an agitated pink, nearly matching the color of her hair. She whispered to attorney Eugene Mc-Pherson, who was assisting her with the case, "I swear, Gene, I didn't know."

On the lighter side, Mrs. Root defended a self-styled Professor of Love who had one avowed purpose in life: to educate American males and females in the delicate art of love-making.

"The Americans make love too impetuously . . . far too fast," the Professor claimed. "They rush through this enjoyable act like they have to hurry to the supermarket and take advantage of a drop in the price of frying chickens."

He had been displaying his techniques in a rented auditorium, aided by a comely blonde assistant. In the audience were vice squad officers, who called the lecture "indecent."

The Professor maintained that the welcoming kiss upon coming home from work should not be a cursory affair between husbands and wives, but a long-drawn-out one of extreme passion that could even lead to the bedroom. It was evident he was overlooking the possibility that a roast might be in the oven.

"Love-making should last from one to three hours," he asserted.

When the snickers of the spectators died away, a wag was

heard to mutter, "That doesn't allow much time for tele-vision."

The judge threatened to clear the courtroom.

Mrs. Root contended the performance of the Professor was "educational."

The jury brought in a verdict of guilty for presenting and performing in an indecent exhibition, and declared that the lecture was of a lewd character.

The judge pronounced sentence of ninety days and placed the defendant on probation for one year.

Mrs. Root had collected only part of her legal fees, but the Professor claimed some money was coming in and promised that at the conclusion of his jail tenure he would discharge his obligation.

He came into the office. "Mrs. Root," he said, "I think you did a capable job of defending me and I wish to pay you."

"I'll be glad to accept," she said.

"Unfortunately," he stated, "the money I expected didn't come through and I'm without funds."

The statement came as not too much of a surprise, and Mrs. Root was prepared to write the case off as a loss. Then the Professor brightened visibly and snapped his fingers.

"There is a way after all that I can repay you."

She waited.

"I'll work out the unpaid balance by teaching you and Mr. Geiger the art of love-making."

Mrs. Root rose from her chair. "Good day," she said icily. "Consider your account paid in full."

8

ANGELS WITH TARNISHED HALOES

Her eyes smolder and her graceful white hands ball into slender fists, which she'll pound on the desk. The air of calmness that usually fits her like a perfectly tailored suit dissipates, and a turbulence vibrates through her body. She is at such times very like a sleek speedboat, motor racing, straining at her moorings.

This violent reaction is predictable whenever a discussion arises about children on the witness stand, a subject which fires Gladys Towles Root with indignation.

She doesn't dislike children simply because they happen to be children. She's a proud grandmother herself, and the chances are that an exploratory trip into her handbag would turn up snapshots of the two youngsters. She abhors certain children, because these children can smash an innocent man's life with the telling of a single glib lie, readily swallowed by a jury.

Carefully groomed for the occasion, faces scrubbed, hair perfectly combed, clothes immaculate, they sit on the stand, all sweetness and cherubic innocence, an imaginary halo shining over their heads—the same halo that sometimes in the course of the trial can become a noose around the neck of the defendant.

She thinks that clever con men are pikers at the art of exaggeration and lying when compared with unscrupulous children. A con man suavely bluffs his lies across; a child, to be believable, simply has to tell one.

"Never under-estimate the gullibility of the jury in a child molestation charge," she lectured to a women's club audience. "We don't get a cross-section. We much too often get a biased panel. There's the usual smattering of housewives and mortgage, insurance, bank and telephone company employees. These larger organizations allow their employees to serve and not suffer penalties in wage losses. Many of them are too young, and a youthful person is prone to presume that nearly everything police officers say is infallible, and that the testimony of a child should be taken literally.

"Personally, I prefer jurors who are over fifty years old. They've had their own ups and downs. They have tolerance and understanding, and have drunk from their own cup of sorrow. They aren't as easily stirred simply because a child is testifying.

"The main reason a child wins over the jury handily is that he creates a false image. They think: the poor, dear, sweet, little thing. How would he ever have known such a sordid experience unless it really happened?

"Well . . . he can. A child possesses an imagination rivaling Alfred Hitchcock's, and often just as macabre. What are their motives for telling the big lie? Usually it's a form of revenge, a personal vendetta. Some are pathological liars. My investigators once uncovered evidence that showed a six-year-old girl had ten men sent to prison before her falsehoods were revealed. In many instances a child is able to supply a vivid description of certain acts of perversion an alleged molester perpetrated on her, because she has been engaging in the same acts long before the alleged molestation.

"Where did they learn their tactics? Television is one place. I don't advocate reaching into the back of the TV set and tearing out the wiring, but I do think a child's viewing should be adult-selected. Not only can they grow up myopic from too steady a TV diet, but they can also grow up with certain values clouded. Too many parents utilize television as a family tranquilizer. The youngsters sit a few feet away from the set, absorbed, quiet. To most parents this is a miracle, anything short of pandemonium in the house being considered a heavenly state of bliss.

"It's true they watch the heroes triumph over the villains. However, the badmen generally reign supreme until the closing scene, and by that time the child might be rooting for them and the damage is done. Life is cheap on the electronic tube circuit, and directors can kill off as many actors as they please as long as they pay them union scale.

"Movies can be an equally bad influence. The adolescent mind retains what is seen on film far better than what the teachers write on school blackboards. One eleven-year-old girl—who is off to a flying start as a fiction writer—saw a motion picture dealing with incest. Subsequently she became angry with her father, using the plot to fabricate a story leading to his arrest.

"I don't pretend to be knowledgeable enough to suggest the necessary nostrums to enable a child today to become a normal adolescent. Yet I do recall that years ago a child had to come home from school at a given time. There was no loitering or the mother was out with a switch in her hand and the lesson of obedience would be emblazoned where it made a lasting impression.

"As the adage goes: 'The hand that rocks the cradle rules the world.' If true, then that same hand should inflict punishment upon offspring when necessary.

"There was a query, half facetiously, half seriously advanced some years ago: 'Are parents people . . . ?' Although children had nothing to do with it getting into print, it did express the juvenile thought of that day. And today the same question is being asked by offspring.

"But, like most phrases that take hold, 'Are parents people?' had something fundamental. And in having something fundamental, it had something of the truth.

"If you analyze, people are plain characters, individuals who are possessed of homely virtues, who understand without the benefit of explanation the facts and foibles of life. Inasmuch as the facts and foibles of life without any garnishment are the meat and drink of juveniles, those who speak their language are the ones they turn to.

"Unfortunately, the average parent doesn't accept things for what they are. If there is ever a question apparently too abstruse, one can always ignore, can't one?

"Understanding of juvenile thoughts and desires is usually too much trouble. So parents become less than people, for people comprehend, and the kids go elsewhere for their explanations. They don't always get the right ones, either.

"For instance, when dinner is over and you're comfortably settled with a magazine or book, do you resent being interrupted with, 'Dad, will you help with this question in my arithmetic?'

"Certainly, if you're even half human you do. But you don't have to show it and mutter something about 'Don't you see I'm busy?'

"Whether you believe it or not, the scheme of things dictates that the development of progeny is more important than your lethargy. People who are broad of vision will forget their own immediate desires for the greater good.

"Nine times out of ten you will find that so-called juvenile delinquents are what they are because they had to turn away from their parents for understanding. Life provides many channels leading from the original source. And, unless the better course is charted, youth's bark is liable to sail into some fetid backwater.

"If you are parents and people, don't worry. If you are parents and can't qualify as people, exercise your minds until the clear thinking begins to show—and help reduce one of the major problems of the day—our juvenile delinquent rate."

Mrs. Root cites an example of the devious way in which a child's mind can work:

There was a handsome young Italian actor, a newcomer to America, who was scheduled to make his initial Hollywood-produced motion picture. Married only two weeks to a beautiful American girl, he started marital life in a Burbank apartment. It was a typical California-type apartment building—about forty units of two stories, semi-circling a swimming pool.

All the windows opened onto the pool. The building had a laundry room, and a bicycle room for children of the tenants. These features were located at the rear of the building near the carports.

On a Saturday evening the police, in answer to a call from the parents of an eight-year-old girl named Shirley, arrived at the apartment. Shirley related the following tale:

"I was with two boys who live here—Mike and Jerry. We wanted to go for a bicycle ride. First I had to go to the laundry room and bring up some clothes to my mamma. There was a man in the room. He was in shorts. He took them down and showed me what he had. I left and told my two friends what happened. We went riding and came back in about an hour.

"When I went to put my bicycle away he was in the room. He said, 'Come here, Sweetie.' I went over to him. He touched himself and said, 'Wouldn't you like to see it grow?' I said that I wouldn't."

"Can you take us to this man?" one of the officers asked.

"Yes," Shirley said. "He lives in apartment eleven."

Shirley's mother, dabbing at her eyes with a handkerchief, said, "He seemed like such a nice man."

"I can hardly believe it," her husband said, shaking his head. "It's hard to understand, Mr. Frascati was always so pleasant and polite."

"We'd like you to sign a complaint," an officer suggested. Shirley's father refused.

"Don't you believe your own daughter?" he was asked.

He paced the floor, distraught. "I just don't want to wreck a man's life. I want to do the right thing, but I'm confused."

The officers argued with him and his wife, to no avail. Finally, they signed the complaint themselves, and accompanied Shirley to apartment eleven. The Frascatis were both in. Apprised of the child's accusation, he screamed and shouted with bursts of uncontrollable rage.

"Ridiculous!" he scoffed. "I never heard of such a thing. I just got married. I love my wife. Why would I do such a thing?"

His wife attempted to pacify him.

Back in her apartment, Shirley added to the incriminating story. She claimed that later, while she was at the swimming pool, he had further exposed himself to her by walking back and forth naked by his window.

Antonio Frascati sought Mrs. Root. They held a lengthy discussion. "Sure I knew Shirley," he readily admitted. "I always thought she was a cute, smart little girl. We usually exchanged a few words whenever we happened to meet around the apartment or pool."

Mrs. Root asked, seeking a motive, "Did you ever have an argument with her . . . do anything to make her angry?"

"Why, no," her client answered. Then he suddenly exclaimed, "Say! Maybe I did. One day we were all playing around in the pool and I ducked her. She was plenty mad. But it didn't seem to last."

"Maybe it lasted longer than you think," Mrs. Root said.

When the trial opened, Mrs. Root thought it strange that the two friends of Shirley, Mike and Jerry, were absent from the courtroom. According to the police reports Shirley had told them about Frascati's actions. This gave rise to Mrs. Root's supposition that they hadn't believed her—otherwise opposing counsel would have them testifying against her client. Or, she wondered, was there a more significant reason? She subpoenaed Mike and Jerry, placing them on the stand. From Jerry she drew a blank. Mike was more productive.

"What were you and Shirley and Jerry doing around the pool that day?" she began.

"Playing games."

"What kind of games?"

"Doctor and patient."

"And you were the doctor?" she assumed.

"Yes."

"Shirley was the patient?"

"Yes."

"Were you playing like you were operating on her?"

"Yes."

"What kind of an operation was it supposed to be?"

The boy said, "We were pretending Shirley was having a baby."

"A baby that you were going to deliver?"

He hesitated, shrugged and said, "Yes."

"That meant that you had to touch Shirley . . . touch her down below when you were play-acting like you were delivering the baby. Isn't that the way it was?"

Mike hung his head and didn't answer.

"Mike," Mrs. Root said, "you're not on trial here. You can tell the truth and nothing will happen to you. You won't be punished." She repeated the question.

"Yes, I did," Mike admitted.

"Touch her?"

"Yes."

"When you finished playing, where did you go?"

He thought a moment before answering, "To the bathroom."

"Did Shirley go in with you?"

"No, she didn't."

"But you wanted her to, didn't you?" Mrs. Root questioned.

"I—I guess so," he said shyly.

Mrs. Root cleared her throat and said, "You asked her to come with you and watch it grow, didn't you, Mike?"

There was no answer.

"You're not on trial, Mike," Mrs. Root reminded the boy again. "You swore to tell the truth. Now isn't that what you said to Shirley?"

"Yes."

When Shirley took the stand, Mrs. Root was astounded by her brazenness. She spoke like an adult. In reference to the male and female organs, she called everything by its proper name. She had been well coached.

Mrs. Root had the court stenographer read back Mike's testimony. "That's where you got the idea to blame it on Mr. Frascati, wasn't it, Shirley?"

"No, it wasn't," denied the child.

Mrs. Root changed the subject. "You didn't like Mr. Frascati, did you?"

"He didn't mean anything to me one way or the other," she retorted.

"Were you ever mad at him?"

"Never," she said emphatically.

"Do you like being ducked in the swimming pool?"

"No."

"How many have ducked you besides Mr. Frascati?"

"Oh, not many, I. . . ." She bit her lip to hold back the words.

"You just admitted Mr. Frascati ducked you."

Her shoulders rose and fell. "I guess he did."

"And you didn't like it, did you?"

"No. Would you?"

Mrs. Root shifted her line of interrogation. "You said in your statement to the police officers that Mr. Frascati exposed himself before you in the window of his apartment when you were at the pool."

"Yes. That's right."

"What were you doing around the pool?"

"Eating lunch."

"It was a hot day, wasn't it?"

"Real hot."

"And on that real hot day, which was Saturday, you saw Mr. Frascati in the window exposing himself to you?"

"Yes. I already told you."

"What time was it?"

"I don't know exactly."

"Would you say it was about noon? Isn't that when you usually eat your lunch?"

"Probably."

"Well now," Mrs. Root said. "It was about noon. It was Saturday and a very hot day. I have the weather reports. The temperature was over one hundred degrees. The pool was crowded. Yet you claim it was solely for your benefit that Mr. Frascati was exposing himself in the window."

"Well, I saw him," the child answered defensively.

"You say that Mr. Frascati first exposed himself to you in the laundry room and then later again in the bicycle room."

"Yes."

"And then he went upstairs when you were eating lunch at about noon and exposed himself from the window?"

"Yes, yes, I told you all that," Shirley said impatiently.

Mrs. Root pointed accusingly at the child, asking, "Then why did you wait from before noon until dinner time to tell your mother and father what happened?"

"What difference does it make?" she blurted.

"That's for the jury to decide."

Shirley said belligerently, "I know what you're going to say."

"What am I going to say?"

"That I had all that time to make up the story before I told my Mamma and Papa."

"Yes, I was. Now didn't you?"

There was no reply.

The jury was out ten minutes. The verdict was acquittal.

What irked Mrs. Root about this case was that it was quite obvious that Shirley's parents thought their child was lying, otherwise they would have signed the complaint willingly. As for the arresting officers, anxious for a case, their hasty action cost the taxpayers of the State of California approximately $2,500 for the trial.

An even greater cost was that suffered by the defendant. He lost his job and all chances at a career which had begun so promisingly. The studio suspended him because the case involved moral turpitude. Whether he was acquitted or not, his arrest is a matter of public record and remains there for the world to know.

Mrs. Root wonders what happens when Frascati seeks another job, and speculates that people will say, "Oh, yes, you were charged with indecent exposure," and he will retaliate by answering, "But I was proved innocent."

"How many will then ask themselves, 'Well, I wonder if the jury didn't make a mistake!' "

And what of Shirley?

"This to me is the saddest part. What becomes of this youngster's integrity, her spiritual evaluation of honesty? What will happen to Shirley when she grows up? Can this leopard change its spots—or will they only grow bigger?"

She contends that in morals offenses juries are incorrect in their verdicts more than fifty percent of the time.

While being interviewed on a television program, Mrs.

Root made the following statement which prompted a flood of letters—the majority in disagreement:

"I believe that a psychiatric examination should be administered to those who report they have been victimized by a sex crime. I urge this because the victim often has deliberately invited the attack or may actually have been the aggressor. Contrary to what many people think, even children are capable of being the aggressor in a perverted relationship with an adult. And there is a shocking number of disturbed youngsters who will frame an adult."

A case that left Mrs. Root with a bitter taste in her mouth involved a narcotics addict. Strongly hooked, he had broken into a drugstore and been apprehended by police before he could steal some morphine which his system craved.

Sent to prison, this man, whose name was Henry Jelk, made a fantastic recovery. Although suffering the tortures of the damned during his withdrawal period at the prison hospital, he kicked himself completely free of the habit. Granted a parole, he came out spiritually well-adjusted and also able to earn a living since he had been trained as a machinist.

His wife, he discovered, had been promiscuous, living with first one man and then another—hardly a fit environment, the court decided when he filed for divorce, in which to rear their ten-year-old daughter, Gwen. He received custody of the child, as he had not only found a job but his mother, recently widowed, had agreed to live with him and aid in bringing up the little girl.

This arrangement was satisfactory to everyone but Gwen. Dwelling with her mother had been a life of pure delight. No restrictions were imposed. She could have ice cream before dinner; she didn't have to keep neat and clean; she could go to bed any hour she chose; and when different men climbed into bed with her mother they would, without exception, tell her how cute and pretty she was. She liked that.

In this new household with her father and her grandmother she lived under a set of rules. Why, she was even forced to attend the Catholic church. At first she rebelled openly. Then, realizing she was getting nowhere, she decided to become submissive and bide her time. Gwen had cunning and patience. An opportunity, she believed, would come her way. When it did, some fertile scheming would free her of her father.

Jelk came in from work one day to be informed by his worried mother that Gwen was long overdue from school. In order to conserve on clothes, it was a must in the Jelk household that Gwen come right home after school and change into bluejeans before going out to play.

Jelk knew she had a companion her own age named Leo, and he walked to the boy's house. The front door was open and he could hear his daughter's voice. He went in. Gwen and Leo were lying on a couch underneath a spread, their bodies pressed together. Jelk jerked his daughter to her feet and hurried her home.

He said to her sternly, "I don't want you ever again to play under the covers with Leo or any other little boy," and, pointing to her privates, asked, "Did he touch you here?"

Gwen whimpered that he hadn't.

Jelk spanked the child soundly, and thought it best to make no mention of what had occurred to his mother, who had been gardening in the backyard.

The next morning after Jelk left for work and his mother was readying the child for school, she noticed Gwen was pouting and asked her the reason.

"My father pulled my panties down and touched me underneath my dress, Granny," she wailed.

"What!" was all her startled grandmother could gasp.

"Yes, yes," the child went on, "and he put his finger inside me."

The older woman collapsed in a chair trying to catch her

breath, panting, "I can't believe it . . . I simply can't believe that your father would molest you."

The child's mind reached out, seized and held onto the word "molest." It was a brand-new word to her, but one she was sure would get her father into trouble.

"Yes," she said gravely, "he molested me, Granny."

That evening the grandmother took Gwen before her son. The child changed her story and told the truth of what actually happened between her and her parent.

Her grandmother pointed out, "You see, Gwen, your daddy didn't molest you. He was instructing you. He only pointed with his finger, and didn't go under your dress."

The child began sobbing. "Yes, that's the way it happened."

Although both Jelk and his mother were upset, they attributed the child's accusations to a "vivid imagination," abetted by "what she must have read somewhere."

The next day Gwen went to the house of neighbors, a childless couple who were crazy about any youngsters and adored Gwen, often giving her candy and cake for the pleasure of her visits. She came straight to the point, declaring, "My daddy molested me," and went into details.

The neighbors called the sheriff's office. Jelk was arrested. Gwen was taken to Juvenile Hall.

The trial opened. Jelk had been continually mentioning a letter he had received from Gwen while he was in jail—a letter, he contended, which might have a telling effect on the trial. He had given it to his mother, who took it home and misplaced it. The evening of the first day of the trial Mrs. Root went to the Jelk house and helped search for the letter. Finally they found it. Jelk, Mrs. Root discovered after reading the childish writing, had not overstated its importance.

When Gwen took the witness stand, she froze. She stared hypnotically at a policewoman. She wouldn't open her mouth.

Mrs. Root pleaded with her. "Now Gwen," she said sooth-ingly, "all you have to do is to tell the truth."

She refused to talk.

Taking from her brief case the letter the child had written, she read aloud the contents:

> Dear Daddy,
> I'm sorry Daddy that I lied. I should have told them that you didn't molest me that you tried to help me. I love you and want you home. I did this because I was mad at you and Mamma said you weren't a nice man and I wanted to go back and live with her.
>
> Gwen

Mrs. Root lowered the letter and asked Gwen, "Did you write this to your Daddy?"

The answer came in the affirmative.

Opposing counsels approached the bench, holding a brief conference with the judge. The case was dismissed.

Commenting on the case, Mrs. Root said, "Here was a child —Gwen—who saw the error in her ways and did something about it in the form of a letter without any prodding. She was repentant. Under the guidance of her father and grand-mother she has an excellent chance of becoming adjusted and leading a normal life."

"Of course," Mrs. Root says, "there's the other side of the fence on this nasty business of child molesting—the legitimate molester, a sexual psychopath. More than seven hundred child-molesting arrests are made in Los Angeles each year, and a great many deservedly so.

"The child-molester is a disturbed man. He can be either married with a family, or single. In a way, he is to be pitied. He has strong guilt feelings and he lives in a private hell within himself. He suffers the torments of the damned and carries a heavy burden of shame.

"Not all molesters are furtive and scheming and feel triumphant when not apprehended by the law. Some have a strong compulsion to be caught . . . they subconciously want to pay for their deviate thoughts and actions.

"Children are everywhere and most of them are approachable, so the molester, who usually bides his time, has a large field for the selection of his intended victim.

"An attack on a child can leave deep emotional scars that can change the course of his or her life. In the parents—before damage can be assayed—the first reaction is horror and often hysteria.

"It is a terrible thing."

The editor of *The Encinian*, a newspaper published at Encino, California, in the San Fernando Valley, once asked Mrs. Root if she would write an article dealing with juvenile deliquency for his publication.

"No," she refused. "I haven't time. But if you have anyone around who can take shorthand, I'll give him something in a few minutes."

A secretary was summoned, and Mrs. Root dictated the following:

"Dependability is a virtue; and, unfortunately, virtues are all too rare these days. Juvenile delinquency is comprised of the lack of many virtues. The lack of dependability is not the least of these.

"In the days of our fathers and grandfathers, the phrase 'His word is his bond' was common. The phrase has become almost obsolete—probably because, regrettably, a man's word has ceased to mean too much. And bonds are seldom what we expect of them.

"Taking this into consideration, it follows that if a man's word isn't worth too much, neither will be his son's nor his daughter's. The children can't be blamed if the example isn't set.

"So, again we return to my major contention: Delinquency is not fundamentally juvenile—it is adult.

"With all our modern conveniences and labor-saving devices, we have too much leisure time. Gradually, over the generations, there have developed too many loopholes for the Devil to get in his hand-work—remembering that 'The Devil finds work for idle hands.'

"Moral fibre has suffered. It has become stupidly 'fashionable' to be late for every appointment . . . to leave important things to the last minute. Children can't help but observe habits of their parents—and if it's good enough for Mommy and Daddy it's good enough for them.

"Thus the virtue of dependability starts its downward course.

"These may seem minor facets of the whole, yet are anything but that. Discipline, the force that makes us do what we know we should when it is easier to do something else, is weakened. The oftener we do the things that are the easiest and slough off obligation, the less strength we have to resist the gay and fascinating visage of temptation. If this seems dramatic, it is only to stress in more lurid form the danger inherent therein.

"The virtue of dependability develops through exercise. If children are taught, not only by words but by example, that dependability is a thoroughly desirable habit and one that pays dividends, it will become a compelling force for good.

"When one is dependable, one considers others. One considers that which is beyond oneself. And so robbery, theft, and all other overt acts that constitute delinquency are automatically labeled 'Unworthy.'

"A parent will go to great lengths to develop a son's physique, or a daughter's musical talent. If one-quarter as much time and thought were devoted to the strengthening of moral fibre, we might have fewer weight-lifters and prospective concert artists, but we would also have fewer inmates of Juvenile Hall—and fewer heartbroken mothers and fathers—and save many broken lives.

"To insure the future of your children, your word must become your bond."

9

NIGHT OF A THOUSAND ROSES

Those who hypothesize that a doctor faces life's problems calmly would have abandoned this generalization had they been present one evening fourteen years ago in the obstetric ward of a top Los Angeles hospital. Here they could see Dr. Jerold B. Rudner, who today handles many surgical cases for Metro-Goldwyn-Mayer, Universal, and Twentieth Century-Fox studios, peering anxiously over the shoulder of a colleague whose attention was focused on the inert figure in the bed.

It was a few minutes past midnight on Mother's Day, and Dr. Rudner's wife had given birth to a baby.

"Why do they always seem to arrive late at night or early in the morning?" Dr. Rudner grumbled as he wiped his perspiration-streaked face.

The telephone rang. Dr. Rudner looked at the instrument dumbly. This tightly-operated hospital had two inviolable rules:

No incoming calls permitted to the OB Ward at this time of night.

No after-hours visitors.

Wondering what catastrophic event short of World War

III could have caused anyone to break the first of those rules, Dr. Rudner picked up the telephone and said, "Hello."

"Hello, young man, what did we have?" came the low-pitched inquiry.

Dr. Rudner gasped. "How did you ever get this call through, Mrs. Root?"

"Never mind that. Just answer my question."

Proudly, the doctor announced, "We had a girl, six pounds, eight ounces."

"Congratulations, I'll be right over."

"Wait a second," Dr. Rudner spoke rapidly before she could hang up. "That's impossible. You can't do it. It's after midnight and the hospital doors are locked. A safecracker couldn't get in here using a blow torch."

The voice at the other end of the wire said, "Don't tell me what I'm going to do. I'll be seeing you."

"But . . ." Dr. Rudner started to protest when he heard the buzzing sound of a broken connection. He repeated the conversation to his friend.

"Is she crazy?" the obstetrician pondered. "Why, I couldn't even get in here at this hour. How can she?"

The hospital Superintendent entered. He was a firm, coldly efficient administrator, who lived by a code of rules. He addressed Dr. Rudner.

"A Mrs. Gladys Towles Root telephoned me," he began.

"Yes, yes," Dr. Rudner said, apologizing. "She's sort of—sort of an eccentric."

"I don't care who she is or what she is," the Superintendent stated with finality. "This is the OB Ward, plus the fact that the hospital is locked. The President of the United States couldn't get in here."

Dr. Rudner replied, "Yes sir, I understand. I tried to tell her."

"I just wanted to make it clear," the Superintendent said haughtily as he left the room.

He reappeared in five minutes. There was something different about him. He reminded Dr. Rudner of a victim of Russian brain-washing who escaped, only later to lose a brief encounter with a steam roller. An air of dejection cloaked him, combined with a humbleness and a patronizing air.

"Doctor," he said, speaking mechanically, "I want to apologize for my brusqueness. Mrs. Root is arriving soon. I'll show her up here myself. Please don't hesitate to let me know if there's anything I can do to make the lady comfortable."

"Just tell me one thing," Dr. Rudner said, bursting with curiosity. "What caused your change of attitude?"

The eyes of the Superintendent dilated with fear. When he spoke his voice trembled.

"I received a telephone call," he said, in hushed tones.

"Another one from Mrs. Root?"

"No. Oh, no. From someone whose name I can't mention. Someone in a very high political position in the State."

"He gave you orders?"

The Superintendent said, "He certainly did. Explicit orders. And he made it clear that any insubordination on my part would cost me my job." He glanced at his wrist watch. "My goodness!" he exclaimed, striding toward the door, "Mrs. Root may be here any moment and I want to be in the lobby to welcome her."

After he left the obstetrician whistled softly and remarked, "She must be quite a woman."

Agreeing, Dr. Rudner volunteered, "She knows where more bodies are buried than you can find in Forest Lawn. I think she has a master key that can unlock every important closet containing a skeleton. She has influence and power to pull any strings."

"She certainly pulled one tonight," the obstetrician chuckled, "and she's also a hypnotist. She changed the Superintendent from a lion into a mouse."

Dr. Rudner's initial introduction to Mrs. Root had come

after he had treated her son Bobby for an overweight condition, taking sixty pounds off the boy. "Young man," she had addressed him, although the age discrepancy wasn't too great, "you've done a fine job on my son. I'd be happy if you'd do some work for me."

The nature of the work was to examine the sex deviates among her clients and submit a report of his findings. After nine years he felt that he knew her pretty well or, as he told his wife, "as well as anyone could know her."

Delighted with his progress, Mrs. Root had promised that someday she would—when she considered him ready for it—build him his own private hospital. He believes that, in time, she will honor her promise.

There were voices in the hallway, and the door to the obstetrical ward opened and Mrs. Root entered. Her appearance was startling. She wore a black suede dress, tightly draped and caught at the hips with two huge gold-and-diamond safety pins. At her throat was a gold choker with her name spelled out in diamonds. Two two-inch-wide gold bracelets studded with pearls dangled from her wrist. A jet-and-amethyst ring measuring three inches across adorned a finger. Jet earrings hung halfway to the collar of a purple-dyed wolf jacket having a bright purple satin lining.

Her hair, under a black fur hat, was red and gold.

She was pushing a baby carriage, of a size that would have held a small dinosaur, containing approximately one thousand Cecil Brunner roses. Following her were Jay Geiger and the Superintendent. Geiger was clad in a white coat, black tuxedo trousers, black velvet slippers.

Perched on his left shoulder was a green parrot.

"Congratulations . . . congratulations . . . congratulations . . ." squawked the bird, ruffling his feathers.

"How do you do, young man," Mrs. Root greeted Dr. Rudner and then, wheeling, she faced the cowed Superintendent to dismiss him with a "You may go now."

The Superintendent slunk from sight.

"Mrs. Root . . ." Dr. Rudner started to protest.

"This will teach him," Mrs. Root stated, "that when I want to see my godchild, there's to be no red tape." Marching to the side of Mrs. Rudner's bed she said, "How do you do, Jean, how are you? We have a fine baby. My congratulations."

Doing an about-face, she strode from the room. Her husband followed. "Congratulations . . . congratulations . . . congratulations . . ." the parrot cried, his voice echoing with the ringing sounds of the lawyer's high heels through the corridor.

The obstetrician dazedly asked, "Did I just have an hallucination, or did I see what I think I saw?"

Dr. Rudner didn't answer. He was busy muttering, "Where at this hour of the night could she get all those roses?"

Since coming to the West Coast and establishing both a professional and a social relationship with Mrs. Root, there has been no chance that ennui could become part of his existence. Her capriciousness and boundless energy amaze him. This poses problems from a doctor's constantly cautious point of view. He worries about her and asks himself questions like: How long can she keep up the pace? When will it begin taking its toll on her?

"She never sleeps enough," Dr. Rudner says. "In fifteen years I've seen her let go only once. That was in Palm Springs. She simply fell apart, sleeping solidly for forty-eight hours. I thought I'd lost her. But come Monday morning she was up bright and early and back in the working saddle again."

Dr. Rudner says that should he have a nightmare, he is certain Mrs. Root would appear as a "smartly-groomed human octopus with dozens of efficient and over-active tentacles all toiling at something unrelated." He calls her a "dreamweaver," explaining that she conjures up wild ones but her dream-making capabilities are unlimited and often as not she makes them come true.

He recalls a summery night when he sought escape from his own personal problems. Without hinting to a living soul where he was going, he got into his car, heading for Zuma Beach—north along the ocean from Santa Monica—to see a couple who had a house high in the hills. Here he was certain he would find the peace and quiet he needed.

Soon after arrival he was chatting with his friends over a cup of coffee, his coat off, tie loosened, and feet propped on a hassock, his worries and tensions easing.

"Boy, do I feel relaxed," he had just sighed, when the doorbell rang.

His host answered it. Outside stood a uniformed sheriff.

"Is Dr. Jerold Rudner here?" asked the official.

With something of an effort, the doctor rose. "I'm Dr. Rudner."

"Would you mind coming with me, Doctor?" the sheriff said. "Gladys Root wants to see you."

Dr. Rudner groaned. "Do I have any choice in the matter?"

"No, sir."

Slipping into his coat, Dr. Rudner asked, "Am I supposed to follow you in my car?"

"No. You leave your car here and ride with me."

"But I'll need my car," the doctor argued.

"Doctor," the sheriff said firmly, "I've got my orders. If I don't bring you in my car, I'll lose my job."

Dr. Rudner bid his hosts goodnight and accompanied the sheriff, who delivered him to Mrs. Root's house. It seemed her husband felt ill. After giving him an injection, he confronted the lawyer.

"How did you find me?"

"Really want to know?"

"Yes, I do. It's harder to escape from you than from Devil's Island."

Mrs. Root said, "I found the address on the pad by the telephone in your apartment."

"But—but," Dr. Rudner stammered, "I might have written that days ago."

"No," Mrs. Root returned, "I conducted my own little test and the ink told me the writing was quite recent."

The explanation apparently satisfied Dr. Rudner until a pertinent thought popped into his head. "I was just thinking," he said, "my apartment was locked. How did you manage to get in?"

"Through connections."

"What kind of connections?"

She said, "You remember the young fellow I got off on a burglary charge last week?"

He nodded.

"Well," Mrs. Root said, "doesn't that answer your question?"

What has specifically impressed Dr. Rudner is the supreme effort by Mrs. Root to save each client, and her display of courage in taking a stand against a judge, which sometimes ends in contempt-of-court charges.

She was trying a case sans jury when she said to the magistrate in reference to the defendant, "He's sick and if you send him to jail you're as guilty as if you put him in the electric chair."

The illustrious Jerry Geisler, who happened to be sitting with Dr. Rudner, whispered, "She frightens me, Doctor. I don't want ever to get up against her. She's got sex and she's got ability and that's a hard combination to beat."

Standing out in Dr. Rudner's memory was the testifying psychiatrist whose findings were in complete disparity with Mrs. Root's line of thinking. She wanted to eliminate his testimony. Her client was a minister who was accused of an act of perversion with his wife. A verdict of guilty, to the delight of a small clique in his congregation, would remove him from the church. Mrs. Root's contention was that a man's home is his castle; a man and woman are one; therefore one cannot commit an act upon oneself.

The psychiatrist had been court-appointed. Mrs. Root cross-examined him until he was nearly ready to lie down on the couch of a colleague. She had prepared herself well by reading many books on the aberration of which her client was being accused. After two hours the psychiatrist was on the verge of a mental crackup. Jumping from the witness stand as if it were a hot seat, he shouted in a strained voice, "I quit! That's all! I quit!"

Staggering from the witness chair, he started to leave the courtroom.

"Just a moment, sir," the judge called after him. "What about your fee?"

"Forget the money," he shouted back. "It isn't worth it."

When the room quieted, Mrs. Root said, "Now we'll produce a psychiatrist with a better nervous system," and she brought forth her own choice.

Possibly the most heated battle of her entire career came in defense of the manager of a large and prosperous and long-established Los Angeles department store. He was a kindly gentleman, a bachelor in his early sixties, a college graduate who on his frequent walks passed a school where he would stop and exchange a few words with the children.

One day he patted a little girl on the head. It proved to be a costly mistake. A busybody with the ability to kick a tidbit of gossip around like a football was scanning the street from a window two hundred feet distant, and called the police, claiming the department store manager had touched the child on her private parts. The police staked out the schoolyard and the next time the man passed, although he merely talked with the child, they picked him up. Police signed the complaint.

The defendant asked for Mrs. Root. He had never been in jail. Two psychiatrists' reports revealed normal tendencies. The judge treated their findings coldly, assuming that the department store manager had ravished the child in broad daylight on the sidewalk.

Staring down from the bench at the defendant, the judge said venomously, "You're garbage. I'm going to see that you get put away for the rest of your life."

It marked one of the few times in her life when Mrs. Root's temper flamed out of control. She fumed and raged, unable to find words to express her feelings. When at last she did, she cried, "You talk like an uneducated, narrow, biased man instead of a judge. This isn't a kangaroo court," she pointed out. "We're not getting a fair trial, but I'll see that we do."

Granted a postponement, she returned to her office and for the better part of an hour kept the telephone wires sizzling. Calls to people in high positions got results. The outcome was a change of venue and ultimate acquittal for her client.

Mrs. Root has been known to toss pointed questions at judges, necessitating recesses until the answers are determined. One such occurrence was in Long Beach, California, where a transvestite had been arrested for the thirtieth time. The prosecutor had dredged up an archaic law concerning transvestitism—that it is permissible for a male to wear women's clothing within his own home, but illegal on the outside.

Mrs. Root based her arguments on the unfairness of the law in this day of single standards. While pleading for her client she noticed the judge unconsciously shaking his head. She understood his thinking: the law is the law no matter how antiquated.

Midway in a sentence she stopped talking, paused for a few seconds, and asked, "Your Honor, can you tell me what's wrong with a man wearing women's clothes if he so chooses?" The headshaking stopped. The judge appeared dumbfounded. He could give no satisfactory answer.

There was one sharp-eyed judge who detected what he thought was a grandstand play employed by Mrs. Root to gain sympathy for her client who was charged with prostitution. The defendant, sitting next to Mrs. Root at the counsel table, was holding her six-month-old baby because, as Mrs. Root asked the court's indulgence, "there was no one to leave it with." Twice during the opening morning session of the trial the baby started to cry, and with each fresh outbreak of wailing the jury gazed tenderly in the direction of the child.

It was during the third crying spell that the judge boomed, "Mrs. Root. I'll have to ask you to refrain from pinching that baby again."

Mrs. Root has made only one appearance before the United States Supreme Court. It was a military case. An argument immediately erupted, not on a point of law but on decorum.

She refused to don the conventional black robes. Argument failed to persuade her. She appeared in a tight-fitting bronze taffeta dress hemmed with brown velvet, bronze ankle-strap shoes, a topaz ring the size of a silver dollar, and a topaz pin of 190 carats at her bust. Over the dress was a monkey-fur cape, all white. Her huge hat was of the same material as the dress and her hair was dyed to match the topaz.

It would be ultra-conservative to state that the dignity of the court was ruffled.

Legal historians believe that this was the only instance since the inception of the U.S. Supreme Court that a woman refused to wear the traditional dress.

After Roby Heard, *Los Angeles Mirror* star writer, wrote a series of articles on Mrs. Root, the lawyer received a large fan mail. Some of the letters criticized her way of life, her style of dress, and the decor of her house and office.

Marjie McNulty was in full support of Mrs. Root's ideas and her right to be an individual. She wrote:

"Thank you a million dollars' worth for permitting the three articles I just read about you to appear in the *Mirror*. Reading them gives me some good memories and a wonderful uplift. It was like inhaling a big breath of lovely fresh air. Even though the writer seems bent on picturing you as a 'Circus Portia' who lives in a peculiarly furnished home, he unwittingly portrayed the woman all of us really want to be. One who dares wear what she pleases when and where she pleases. And to furnish her home as she and her husband really want it, and not as custom dictates.

"It was so refreshing, reading about you—and realizing that the story between the lines is really true. There are still people in the world who are free individuals in spite of mass pressures and you are one of them."

Mrs. Root showed the letter to Dr. Rudner. "Well expressed," he commented, and with a twinkle in his eye he said, "it shows you have a fan club numbering at least two. I'm the other member."

Dr. Rudner, aided by years of experience in psychiatric probings, is perhaps the one person who can gaze fluoroscopically inside the character of Mrs. Root. He says, "During trials she may seem hard and merciless. But this is only a veneer. Actually she is soft as butter. All her thoughts slope toward the humane side. She'll take off her gloves and fight for the rights of a social outcast.

"Crowding the jail every day are recidivists who have known her for twenty years. Jail is a second home for them. Frequently I have seen Mrs. Root go into the jails with a money-stuffed purse and, moving from cell to cell, distribute the contents to the inmates.

"When asked, 'Won't they just blow it on liquor when they get out?' she admits that they probably will, but says, 'Maybe just one of the many will put it to constructive use—and I consider putting food in their stomachs constructive—and then I would feel rewarded.' "

The snap judgment of many labels Mrs. Root, due to her eccentricities and bizarre dress, an extrovert. On this subject Dr. Rudner says, "Decidedly no." He acknowledges that undoubtedly she's part actress, but her general demeanor is pathological and slightly schizophrenic.

"Whatever happened in her early life to make her this way, I'm uncertain," is his opinion. "Whatever it was, a steam shovel couldn't dig it up. Perhaps," he ventures a guess, "it started after her father died. He was a firm-fisted, high-principled, conventional man and possibly when he died she let out her feathers.

"She has saved thousands from prison and those she has saved have attached themselves to her with a fanatical, slavish devotion that is going to last as long as they live."

10

NURSES INSTEAD OF GUARDS

The telephone is a handy instrument often credited with the saving of lives. Dialing it any hour of the day or night can summon the police, fire department, an ambulance, or Gladys Towles Root, attorney. The arrival of any of the aforementioned automatically places the distressed caller in capable hands.

It is a source of some annoyance to the telephone company that the unlisted number is fast becoming a status symbol. With the subscriber demanding more protection from solicitors, the digits are guarded with the importance of secrets of state.

Not so with Mrs. Root. Her home number—WEbster 4–3104—is listed in the Central Directory, available to one and all. It rings incessantly. Never is the line busied by idle chitchat or trivialities. Time is too precious. Callers, many with desperation in their voices, come directly to the point:

"Mrs. Root . . . I'm in trouble."

"I'll do what I can," she reassures, reaching for a gold pencil and a pad. Before the conversation is terminated, the telephone line has expanded to the size of a lifeline and the client-to-be feels that he is already being pulled toward safe ground.

Endless variety marks the calls. They may range from a narcissist to a fetishist, an exhibitionist, a masochist, to the more prosaic man or woman wishing to shed a mate. All are emotionally disturbed persons requiring help.

Why do hundreds of arrested sexual deviates seek Gladys Root?

A university-educated convicted morals offender explained it this way:

"Being a social outcast, my feelings have been acutely developed to the point of sensitiveness where I am aware of hostility bristling toward me from a prejudiced person. In the presence of Mrs. Root I can sense an inherent sympathy, tenderness, and understanding of my problem. There is also a spiritual quality coming from her. I can discuss my weaknesses with her unashamedly. She calls my abnormal behavior a sickness and speaks of a cure.

"Another reason that I want her in my corner is that she's a damned fine lawyer."

It is within the office of Mrs. Root that deviation from the sexual norm, a topic kept too often in the dark, bursts into light. Here, as the lawyer faces her client, she tries, before hearing the charges and taking a statement or mapping the defense, to gain the fullest confidence.

Many of her cases come from the Hollywood area, where the voice of that city, the *Hollywood Citizen-News*, claims that "one out of every fifteen men you pass on the streets is a sexual deviate."

The Hollywood police vice detail records indicate there are between 10,000 and 20,000 sex deviates in Hollywood, and that between ten and fifteen percent of the male population is homosexual. Arrests from this city include state employees, a Municipal Court clerk, a college professor, high school teachers.

"These people need help," Mrs. Root states. "Contrary to

what some think, cure of the deviate is highly possible. Less than two percent are born that way.

At times as high as fifty percent of the inmates of the Atascadero State Hospital at Atascadero, California, are clients of Mrs. Root who have been sent there by the courts for observation and treatment, recommended after examination by her own or State-appointed psychiatrists. Each time a client journeys to Atascadero it is another victory for Mrs. Root.

One of her principal problems is convincing deviates of their need for treatment. Tremendous resistance is often encountered. "You are sick," she impresses upon them. "You have broken the laws of God, man, and nature. You need help."

Most lawyers fluff off the moral side and justify taking a client whose guilt seems manifest by using the cliché that everyone is entitled to a trial. Mrs. Root, who can establish more rapport with a client in five minutes than an ambassador could with a foreign diplomat in five days, will say, "I don't want to hear about what you did or didn't do. Let's first of all learn what's made you ill. You will see my doctor or my psychiatrist and you will not worry."

This gambit can remove all thorns that might stick in an attorney's conscience.

After consultation, her dominant personality provides an emotional catharsis. Clients often exhibit initial hysteria, induced by stress and strain: "You get me out . . . I'll pay you anything . . . just get me out!" But their anguish soon becomes controllable.

Mrs. Root has come off with flying colors in the majority of her statutory rape cases. Such offenses usually involve men in the forty- fifty- sixty- and occasionally seventy-year-old brackets, who have allegedly attacked an underage girl. In the parlance of the courtroom loungers—persons with time on their hands who enjoy free drama—"she walks them out the front door."

Here are some excerpts from a case handled by Mrs. Root, in which a girl of seventeen claimed she had been raped by a man of sixty-eight.

MRS. ROOT, *addressing judge:* Your Honor, I want you to take a look at this young lady and at my client. Do you think that while he's approaching her with what he's got in mind he's concerned about her birth certificate? You know it's an anatomical fact that when the blood is in the pelvis it can't be in the brain.

MRS. ROOT, *sweetly, to Plaintiff:* I'm a woman and you're a woman and the judge will always be your father, so let's be very honest. You mean to say that at no time did you ever indicate to this man that you were willing?

GIRL: No.

MRS. ROOT: Do you dress to appeal to men?

GIRL: No.

MRS. ROOT: Never with that in mind?

GIRL: No.

MRS. ROOT: I notice your dress is up rather high and that you're wearing stockings. Are you wearing stockings to hide varicose veins?

GIRL: No, I don't have varicose veins.

MRS. ROOT: Is it because they make your legs look pretty?

GIRL: Yes.

MRS. ROOT: If they make your legs look pretty, then you must look pretty to that man there [*indicating the defendant*]. Isn't that correct?

GIRL: Yes.

MRS. ROOT: You just told me that you don't dress to appeal to men.

GIRL: (No answer.)

MRS. ROOT: You're wearing a tight skirt, an off-shoulder dress, a type of brassiere pushing your breasts up. Isn't that dressing for a man?

GIRL: (No answer).

By this time the judge has usually reached a decision. Mrs. Root, in resting her case, makes her customary statement: "We will wait outside while you're deciding, Your Honor," and then she leads the defendant by the hand from the courtroom.

In her preachments on maladjustments of the sexual life, in which satisfaction is sought in aberrant ways, Mrs. Root states that environment is a major contributing factor. She favors an extensive program of sex-crime prevention through sex education, contending, "This training should begin very early in childhood as a natural and logical part of instruction in everyday living. Each youngster should be taught that his private parts are as God-given as his arms and legs. I feel that a community which fails to undertake meaningful sex education becomes an accomplice in the development of perversion.

"One city that is on its toes regarding sex education, although the problems are not of large proportions, is Inglewood, California, an unincorporated community close to Los Angeles. As a preventive measure in combating child-molestation, the Inglewood Police Department in conjunction with the Inglewood School Board and Sid Davis Productions of Hollywood have produced a series of education films available for showing to school children.

"Titles of these films are 'Girls Beware,' 'Boys Beware,' 'Terrible Truth,' 'Seduction of the Innocent.' Among other films produced by Davis concerning child-molestation and designed for youths from grammar school through high school are, 'Dangerous Stranger,' 'Strangers,' and 'Name Unknown.'"

She points out that "the transition for a citizen from freedom to jail is swift as lightning and can happen undeservedly to any innocent bystander caught in a tangled web of circumstantial evidence abetted by lies told by a juvenile; and then the doors of your former happy life can shut for an untold number of years and a brand is stamped on you forever."

She warns, "Be careful around children. Any well-adjusted person can find himself in jail tomorrow for exhibiting over-friendliness with a child."

The intent of a trial by jury is simple: to discover the truth. But the road traveled to arrive at a conclusion is serpentine and often treacherous. It is booby-trap-lined, filled with numerous detours, blind alleys, and false directional signs.

Mrs. Root was one of the first lawyers to recognize the worth of psychiatric examinations for morals offenders. She has avoided trials and thus saved the State of California millions of dollars in court costs when her doctors' reports have been accepted in hearings.

11

HE SANG A CRADLE SONG

There's hardly a day in Los Angeles when someone, voicing a complaint as he struggles to down the flavorless food served in a nondescript hash house, isn't squelched by the remark: "Where do you think you are anyway—Perino's?

Perino's, located on Wilshire Boulevard, has gained lasting fame through the years as a purveyor of fine comestibles and potables. The chef receives an executive's salary. Some of the maitre d's, captains, and waiters have retired to manage their real estate holdings and study the *Wall Street Journal*. It would not be uncommon to find the parking lot boys on vacation registered in one of Las Vegas' expensive hostelries.

There was an untrue rumor not long ago that Perino's was going to the dogs, catering to the *hoi polloi*. It started when Alex Perino, the owner, as a special concession, priced a Thanksgiving dinner at twelve dollars. This was considered cut-rate eating at an á la carte establishment where a plate of soup is one dollar and twenty-five cents, bread and butter seventy-five cents, a pot of coffee eighty cents and a single diner's tab—with a bottle of vintage wine—once totaled two hundred and eleven dollars.

The carriage trade of Perino's has included visiting royalty, foreign diplomats, ambassadors, statesmen, and the usual charge-account patrons from Pasadena, San Marino, and Santa Barbara society. The environment is sedate, the décor richly conservative. Perino's has no music, no entertainment, no blatancy. It concentrates on cuisine and service. To allow a water glass to remain unfilled would be calamitous. A dropped plate—against which the odds are a million to one—never breaks, simply nestling against the thick nap of carpeting.

It was into this atmosphere that Mrs. Root and her husband Jay Geiger made a startling entrance for luncheon in 1946, the exact date of which the restaurant management would, if they only could, be happy to forget. The lawyer was clad in a purple velvet dress with twenty yards of skirt and scalloped hemline and sixty yards of tulle petticoat underneath. She carried a matching velvet purse two feet square. Her earrings were shaped to resemble bunches of lilacs. Two additional clusters of lilacs adorned one of her oversized hats. Her jacket was dyed purple and her shoes matched. Her hair was strawberry blonde.

Mr. Geiger wore a vicuna suit. The jacket lapels were mink, as were all buttons on the jacket and trousers. His cufflinks were also mink. On his left shoulder rode Pablo, the green parrot from the jungles of Brazil, a bird—at least up until that afternoon—of impeccable manners and an expert's knowledge of opera. Without encouragement he would sing arias from all the famous ones.

The threesome was escorted to a booth. One of the diners, who was spooning up a plateful of soup, unconsciously placed a guarding hand over the accompanying crackers as the bird passed his table. It was a needless gesture. Pablo, before many minutes elapsed, would have far meatier cravings.

The bird was humming a few bars from *Rigoletto*, which prompted Geiger to mention, "Pablo seems sad today."

Mrs. Root, who was carefully seating herself over the many

yards of material, composing her dress, replied, "He may perk up before the afternoon's over."

A more oracular statement was never made.

Geiger, studying the menu, was making selections for his wife. The ordering was always left in his experienced hands. As he was discussing the merits of partridge sauté *au rissotto* as opposed to buttered shrimps *en croustade*, Pablo hopped off his shoulder, ruffled his feathers, and carefully worked his way toward an adjoining booth occupied by a dignified couple.

"Pablo, come back here," Geiger called.

The voice of his master failed to discourage the bird from the devilment in mind. Above a white collar protruding from a dark coat was an expanse of unprotected neck—the clean, scrubbed neck of a gentleman—the objective of the parrot. Stealthily he crept along the back of the booth and, moving in for the kill, sank his sharp beak into tender flesh.

There was a startled roar of pain; a woman screamed; blood spurted, crimsoning the collar. Hastily retreating to his owner, Pable burst into the gay strains of *The Marriage of Figaro*.

The wounded man, staggering to his feet, clutched a handkerchief to his perforated neck and swung around to face Mr. and Mrs. Geiger and his feathered tormentor. His gaze centered on Mrs. Root.

"My God," she mumbled, recognition dawning, "of all people."

Before her husband could question her, the stricken victim, his handkerchief bloodied like the battle standard of a defeated nation, stormed from the dining room, his wife trailing behind him.

"You know him?" Geiger asked his wife.

"Know him," she repeated hollowly. "He's the Superior Court judge who found my client guilty in a morals case yesterday!"

Geiger extracted a cigarette from a solid gold case, lit it with a ruby-encrusted lighter, and blew a smoke ring into the air. "Wow!" he said softly.

Shaking her head hopelessly, Mrs. Root moaned, "The judge'll never believe we didn't train Pablo to bite him."

"It was destiny," Geiger returned, and after thinking a moment he added, "or retribution for his court ruling."

If the marriage between Gladys Root and Jay Geiger wasn't made in heaven, it was surely as close to it as two humans without benefit of space-craft can soar. They were were supremely happy.

His wife described Geiger as having a "baby face, beautiful eyes and eyelashes." He stood six feet one inch, with broad shoulders and a tapered waist. His hair was black and very straight.

His mode of dress was every bit as individualistic as his mate's. While the contents of his roomy closets might have had a traumatic effect on conservatives, causing occasional tongue-waggings about a "cross between a minstrel man's apparel and a costume for a fancy dress ball," on Jay Geiger the clothes seemed fitting and proper.

Not only did he always wear a hat—an anomaly under the kind skies of Southern California—but he knew what to do with it in the presence of a lady. His mere doffing, accompanied by a courtly bow, especially before older women, stirred their sluggish blood with youthful memories.

Looking every inch an English gentleman "born to the purple" (which, of course, was his wife's favorite color), Geiger's manners were Chesterfieldian and his social proprieties a page torn from Amy Vanderbilt's book on etiquette. He generally carried an English cane or a walking stick, gracefully maneuvered. His humor, easy temper, and soft-tongued amiability made him a man impossible to hold in contempt. Only a few arguments ever upset the even tempo of his existence and in each case, the adversaries were laughing within a few minutes.

Geiger, like his wife, was partial toward massive, custommade, colorful jewelry. His Swiss-purchased wrist watch was four inches in diameter, with a half-inch-thick gold band. He wore a companion wedding ring to his wife's amethyst with onyx on top and diamond crosses sunk into the sides.

"Jay could perform artistic miracles with hands," recalls Mrs. Root. "One day I saw a beautiful tropical flower in a store and I just happened to mention that I wished I had some artificial copies of it. The next thing I knew, he had examined the flower and made me a dozen. They appeared fully as lifelike as the original. He even created petals, covering my shoes with them, using pearls in the center like a dewdrop."

After they moved into the huge house on Muirfield Road, the couple decided to hold a Christmas party (which later became an annual affair). They worked laboriously to ready the manse for the holidays. Geiger had a flair for the modern mixed with Victorian and English, plus a love for French mirrors.

Two thousand invitations were mailed for the party. The night before, there were no coffee tables on which to serve the food, no lamps. Everything had been promised, but nothing had arrived. Geiger had entwined the staircase to simulate a Christmas tree, with strings of colored lights climbing to the top, where sat an enormous Santa Claus.

At four o'clock on the afternoon of Christmas Eve he telephoned his wife, who was just leaving the office for the hairdresser's, and broke the news that the furniture and lamps hadn't been delivered.

"Darling," he calmly informed her, "I'm down on my hands and knees scrubbing the lanai. The housekeepers didn't show. We have hardly any lights."

"Any suggestions?" Mrs. Root wanted to know.

"I guess maybe we could line up the guests and give each of them a candle as they come in."

"Be sensible," she begged.

"Okay," he replied. "You go out and buy fourteen coffee tables and lamps. The stores are still open."

"Are you serious?"

"I certainly am."

"I'll try," Mrs. Root concluded.

She drove up Washington Boulevard, stopping at a furniture store. It was almost five-thirty. Asking to see the manager, she came instantly to the point:

"I need fourteen coffee tables and fourteen lamps."

He nodded. "We can accommodate you. Just when would you like them delivered?"

"Right away."

The manager gasped. "Madam," he said, "I'll have to order them from the factory."

"I want them immediately," Mrs. Root insisted, explaining her plight and adding, "The lamp shades must be pink, green, and black."

"I can't possibly fill the order," he said shaking his head.

Mrs. Root seized him by an arm. "Come on," she ordered, "we'll walk through the store and look through the warehouse."

They walked. They looked.

Fourteen tables were finally unearthed, as were the lamps. However, the lamps were the wrong colors. Also, the delivery truck was locked in the garage and the driver had left for the day.

"You have a truck outside?" the manager asked hopefully.

"I have a Cadillac sedan."

"It isn't large enough."

"I know," Mrs. Root agreed. "I'll call my husband. He may have some ideas!"

She explained the predicament to him. He said that he'd

use the green, fast-drying paint he sprayed on the Christmas tree to change the color of the lamp shades.

"It's a cinch," he said.

"Good," Mrs. Root was happy. "Now what about getting the tables home?"

"I'll leave that up to your ingenuity," Geiger said.

"But just how, Jay?"

"You'll figure out some way," he said confidently.

She hung up slowly, her mind working feverishly. Her eyes strayed to the store window and through the plate-glass she saw, stopped at a traffic light, the delivery truck of a nationally-known store. Holding up her wide skirts to enable her to get more speed, she ran out the door and began screaming at the truck driver to stop.

He leaned down from the cab seat:

"You sick, lady? Injured? You wanna go to a hospital?"

"No, no," she said positively. "I need your truck."

"Sorry, lady," the driver answered, anxious to get away as he noted that the light was changing.

Mrs. Root cried desperately, for want of a better reason, "I have a charge account at your store."

The driver shrugged. "So what? You can't charge no truck, lady."

Twisting the handle to open the cab door and paying no heed to the honking of horns behind, she babbled out her story, pleading. "Can't you please help me?"

"I ain't no Santa Claus, lady," the driver grumbled.

Mrs. Root opened her handbag, extracting a wad of crumpled bills. "But I am," she stated.

"Climb in," the driver said, his eyes widening.

They rode to the back of the furniture store, where they loaded the tables and lamps. "Not a word about this, lady, or I'll lose my job," he cautioned her.

"Not a word," she agreed, holding a finger against her lips.

Taking no chance of a mistaken address, Mrs. Root had her

chauffeur drive the car home, while she rode alongside the truck driver to direct him to her house. Parked outside the rear door, they began unloading. Jay Geiger appeared in a sweatshirt and denim trousers. Perspiration dripped from his brow. He did not seem at all surprised, having taken it for granted that his wife could accomplish the impossible.

A frenzy of work followed. Then Mrs. Root and her husband fairly threw on their clothes. Timed with the final zip of her dress, the front doorbell rang, heralding the arrival of the first guests.

It was a gala affair. Strolling musicians and singing waiters livened up the party. Many were the compliments for the tablecoths, made by Mrs. Root out of silver netting. Rhinestone stars were sewed into the flounces, providing a glittering effect to blend with the silver and pink dining room.

The party, lasting until seven in the morning, cost—counting individual gifts—$30,000, plus an unlooked-for expense: thievery to the tune of an additional $5,000 and scattered vandalism. Even the rhinestones had been torn from the tablecloths by souvenir-hunters. Numerous articles of clothing were missed from closets that had no locks on the doors. In the bedroom, someone with muddy shoes had walked over the white satin coverings of the pulled-together twin beds.

The last guest to depart was a woman employed in the courthouse. She claimed that the coat hanging in the closet—and it was bare save for this one—didn't belong to her.

"Mine was a Persian lamb," she insisted.

Mrs. Root's personal maid drew her aside, whispering, "I remember her coat when she came in. It was camel's-hair."

Placating the guest, Mrs. Root said she'd telephone her before the day was over. Then she searched the pockets of the coat, and found a monogrammed white lace handkerchief with initials that matched the name of the guest.

Employing tactics she could have borrowed from one of

her trial defenses, Mrs. Root called the woman and said, "We didn't find your coat, but we found a handkerchief of yours."

"Oh," the woman mused, asking, "What kind is it?"

"It has a blue border and is uninitialed," Mrs. Root told her.

"That isn't mine," the woman said. "Mine was white lace with my initials.

Mrs. Root said casually, "Yes, I know."

After a few seconds of silence the voice at the other end of the line inquired, "How do you know?"

"Because it was in the pocket of *your* camel's-hair coat," Mrs. Root returned sharply.

"I—I guess I—I made a mistake," the woman stammered. "You know how it is when a person drinks too much."

Mrs. Root said, "I wouldn't know. I don't drink. Your coat will be sent to your apartment within the hour."

Despite losing some faith in human nature, the Geigers continued the gala parties each year. But at each subsequent party detectives mingled with the guests and attendants handed out coat checks. So famous did the annual affair become that those receiving invitations found that they could sell them for as high as a hundred dollars.

A few days after the holidays, Geiger asked his wife if she didn't want to see a nationally-known magician who was performing on a Los Angeles stage.

"I don't believe so," Mrs. Root decided. "I've already seen a camel change into a Persian lamb and back again into a camel within the space of a few hours. No magician can top that."

Mrs. Root surprised her husband on one of his birthdays by presenting him with a white monkey named Charley. She dressed him in a sports jacket, top hat and striped trousers. The animal had belonged to a circus clown, who sold it to an organ grinder, who sold it to Mrs. Root. The organ grinder probably retired a wealthy man, because Charley had an incurable habit of going through a person's pockets and stealing valuables.

"He'd make a good client for you," Geiger told his wife.

"I have enough repeat offenders now," she said.

The monkey was crazy about Geiger and would bring him all pilfered articles, which kept him busy returning them. Although the next-door neighbors were banana lovers, they seldom managed to enjoy the fruit. Charley saw to that. He would surreptitiously enter the house by raising a bathroom window and, once inside, he would make directly for the fruit bowl, gobble the bananas, and leave the peelings.

Charley finally went the way of all meddlesome monkeys: to the zoo.

Mrs. Root and her husband were constantly giving each other animals—a steady procession of peacocks in diapers, lambs, dogs, cats, rabbits dressed in Easter regalia. They were a continuous source of delight to the children.

During a discussion on the immortality of the soul, Mrs. Root said that if reincarnation wasn't just a nebulous theory, she'd like an earthly return wearing a white dress and riding upon the back of a winged elephant.

On the morning of her birthday a steam calliope stood outside the house, awakening the entire neighborhood with a cacophonous rendition of "Happy Birthday." She opened the front door. There stood an elephant with cardboard wings.

"Happy birthday and happy reincarnation!" shouted Jay Geiger.

She threw her arms around her husband.

"Ride him," he encouraged.

"But I don't have the proper white dress."

"See your dressmaker then," he advised.

"It would take too long to design one."

"You know the life span of an elephant," Geiger reminded. "I'm sure he'll still be around."

Three days later a child living in the Hancock Park section came running into the house shouting, "Mummy! There's a lady in a white dress riding a big elephant by the house and the elephant has wings!"

The child's mother smiled understandingly and mumbled to herself: "Children—what fantastic imaginations they have."

The Los Angeles street-cleaning department would have argued that point.

It was four A.M.

Mrs. Root stirred and awakened from deep sleep. She felt uneasy. Something had roused her and she didn't know what it was. She hadn't been dreaming. She listened . . . hoping for a clue. It came, in the terrifying form of a low moan. Her body snapped into a rigid upright position as she turned on the light, her eyes searching her husband's bed.

Empty.

Again she heard the disturbing sound, an implication of dire suffering that seemed to float on the air, coming from behind the closed door of her husband's dressing room. He was sick, she knew, and out of consideration for her had tried to soundproof his agony by sealing it off behind the thick dressing room door. She remembered what he had once told her: "You need your sleep more than I do. You get precious little of it. I don't want anything short of fire or earthquake to disturb you."

She swept back the bedclothes and raced to the dressing room. Jay Geiger sat slumped in a chair, head bent, hands covering his face.

"Jay," she whispered.

Slowly he withdrew his hands, raising his head. His face was ashen. "Pain," he gasped. "Stomach. Tried home medication. Nothing helps."

"I'll call a doctor."

The doctor came quickly. An ambulance was ordered and the stricken man sped to a hospital, where injections of morphine were given to ease his suffering. After X-rays were taken, nine surgeons studied them. A difference of opinion arose. Some diagnosed the trouble as an acute pancreatic condition, favoring an immediate exploratory operation. Others suggested waiting.

Mrs. Root thought of a hung jury.

She conferred with her husband. He proposed, "Let's wait a bit and first try spiritual aid."

Two Christian Science practitioners visited him. Three hours passed and Geiger said to his wife resignedly, "I'd rather be dead than suffer any more."

He was wheeled into surgery.

The operation lasted five hours. Mrs. Root had given explicit instructions: "I want to see every surgeon after the operation." Seven of the nine surgeons were waiting for her after Geiger was wheeled into his private room. They had found a pancreatic cyst containing fluid, which they drained.

The lawyer accepted their report without comment. Then she asked, "Where are the other two doctors?"

"It's their custom," explained a colleague, "to leave after their work is done."

"And it's my custom to be able to speak with surgeons after operations," she countered.

She sent for the hospital Superintendent, telling him, "Either the two missing doctors return and talk with me or they can keep their bill."

They showed within the hour.

Geiger spent six weeks in the hospital. He was never completely free of pain. Mornings after court Mrs. Root would sit with him, leave for the office, and return for the changing of his private nurses.

Attached to his nose was a post-operative Levine nasal gastric suction tube. Should it, by any chance, fail to function, the patient would become violently ill. One day as Mrs. Root came down the hospital corridor, she noticed the emergency light on over his door. She found the machine not working, the nurse asleep, and her husband unconscious.

She aroused the Superintendent who called a staff doctor. Geiger was revived. Upon being discharged from the hospital, he returned home to continue recuperation but it was deemed necessary to have around-the-clock nursing.

The hospital and doctor bills came in. In Mrs. Root's own words, "They thought they had a bank for a patient."

Geiger was slow to show improvement. At night the pains worsened. Morphine dosages were increased. Often around three or four o'clock in the morning it was necessary to summon a doctor. Seventy-five dollars was the price of a night call. Additional medical consultations were held. From them came a diagnosis that another pancreatic cyst had formed.

Another operation followed. Surgeons told Mrs. Root they drained a quart of fluid. A biopsy revealed no malignancy. Geiger rallied slowly and at length came home. The nurses were continued. New drugs were tried. Doctors came in and out of the Hancock Park house almost hourly.

Geiger was depressed and he aired his despondency to his wife. "No one is managing the home, the office, or the children," he complained. "I want to be useful—not just lie here helplessly. I'm placing too much burden on you."

Pneumonia set in. Cornering one of the physicians, Mrs. Root asked for an explanation. Blame was placed on the nurses. "They didn't move him enough—left him too dormant," the lawyer was told.

One morning while in the midst of dressing to go to the office, Mrs. Root was called by the nurse, who said, "I've discovered something and I think we'd better send for the doctor at once."

"What is it?" Mrs. Root questioned.

"I'll show you," the nurse said. She opened Geiger's pajamas. Six inches of gut hung out. Mrs. Root weaved from the room and vomited. Upon recovery, she telephoned the surgeon who had performed the last operation.

He diagnosed, "It's evident the sutures haven't healed and the tissue gave way. We'll have to bring him back to the hospital and sew him up again."

She was assured that within a few days her husband would be home. For what began as a simple re-suturing Geiger spent six hours on the operating table. The consensus was pessimistic: he still showed a pancreatic condition that was beginning to affect the liver.

He then went into jaundice.

Geiger returned to the house four weeks later after numerous blood transfusions. Every two hours he received narcotic pain killers. Now in his second year of sickness he had a lung specialist, a heart specialist, a kidney specialist. His gall bladder was bad and it was believed that he was becoming diabetic. His screams filled every night, echoing through the big house. Another operation was advised. At this time, Mrs. Root was attempting to concentrate on some of the heaviest trial work in her career.

She received some counsel from one of the doctors, who said: "You and your husband have something wonderful—a deep, unbreakable love bond. It's Siamese twin-like. If one half fails, the other half fails. You, Mrs. Root, are the live half. The other half must feed and be dependent upon you to keep life flowing."

She asked, "What can I do? Tell me and I'll do it."

"You must be gay around Mr. Geiger, even if your heart is heavy. You must never shed a tear before him. Keep up a front at all times. Dress to please him. Consult him about household and business matters. Make him feel useful. At the end of each day tell him how well the work went. Keep bubbling with enthusiasm."

She discussed the operation with her husband. He shook his head in protest. "Not another hospital. I'd rather bow out of this world first."

Mrs. Root had a sudden thought. "Jay—suppose we fix up the master bedroom as an operating room. I'll move in Klieg lights. I'll duplicate operating room equipment."

"Is that the way you want it?" he asked.

"I think it is, Jay."

"Let's give it another try then," he consented.

The operation accomplished nothing. He still had the same pains, same swelling in the abdomen, same general complaints. If anything, the pains were sharper.

"They stab me like knives," he muttered.

It was while in court pleading a case that Mrs. Root felt it tugging at her. "A giant magnet came to mind," she recalled. "It seemed to be trying to pull me from the courtroom." The feeling obscured her legal thoughts and her voice faltered. She felt she must yield to it, nebulous as it might be. A whispered conference with the judge followed. He granted a postponement.

Her chauffeur under instructions to "ignore the speed laws," the white Cadillac streaked toward Hancock Park. Bounding up the stairs to her husband's room, she found Geiger in bed snoring. The nurse was, she presumed, somewhere in the house. Everything appeared in peaceful order and she was beginning to think that the intuitive flash received in the courtroom was false.

As she stood for a moment, catching her breath and orienting herself, a feeling of alarm pricked at her. Then she knew what was wrong: his snores. They were labored, heavy, unnatural. At his bedside she examined his face. It was a blue shade. By the bed she spied a cocktail glass containing a fragment of melting ice. The doctors permitted an occasional creme de menthe over ice, believing it might act as a stomach-settler.

Then she saw something that caused her heart to pound. On the table an empty bottle lay on its side. With trembling fingers she picked it up. The inscription told her it had once contained one hundred three-quarter-grain Nembutols. The date revealed that the prescription had been filled only the day before.

There was no doubt what he had done: swallowed nearly one hundred of the tablets with a creme de menthe chaser—truly a cocktail of death.

The nurse came in. Her eyes dilated with surprise at seeing Mrs. Root, who screamed, "Where have you been?"

"I've only—only been away from the room a short time," she replied, badly frightened.

"That short time may cost my husband his life."

She grabbed the telephone, called the doctor and the fire department. They came quickly, followed by newsmen and photographers. Two firemen worked with a respirator. After two hours and fourteen minutes, Geiger was pronounced out of danger.

The doctor announced he was withdrawing from the case and taking his associates with him. Mrs. Root stared at him. "What's your reason?"

He shrugged. "A psychiatrist might serve the purpose," he said enigmatically, declining further discussion.

She had been through a small army of doctors. Racking her brain, she thought of Dr. Rudner. He might be able to help where high-powered specialists had failed. She sought his help.

Dr. Rudner examined Geiger. His discovery was frightening. "Mrs. Root, it seems that your husband has been on morphine for nearly three years, at intervals of two hours. Do you realize the significance of this?"

She didn't answer.

He launched into an explanation, concluding with, "Mr. Geiger is, to put it bluntly, an addict. In plain words, he's hooked—hooked so badly I can't even distinguish clearly among his symptoms of illness."

Mrs. Root had been standing. She groped for a chair and almost fell into it. "What can we do, Doctor?"

He sighed. "I would suggest a gradual withdrawal, rather than a sudden one. It's going to be torturous. I'll leave the decision to you."

"If it has to be done, it has to be done," she decided.

Narcotic reductions began. Three male nurses were hired on eight-hour shifts. The suffering became intense. Geiger's once finely-proportioned body shriveled as the pounds dropped away.

On a Friday, despite an unusually heavy schedule, Mrs. Root went back to check on her husband's condition four times during the day. That night an urgent call sent her downtown again to the office. It was nearly eleven o'clock when she was able to conclude her business and start for home.

The house was unusually still. As she opened the door to her husband's room, a sight greeted her that will remain with her for the rest of her years. Jay Geiger was climbing out an open window. Around his neck was a knotted, twisted bed sheet tied to another one and secured to a bedpost. The bed had been pushed close to the window.

"Normally," she recalled when that frightful day was long over, "I'm not an especially strong person. But on this occasion strength came from sheer emotion and determination. Jay was half-way out the window when I reached him. I wrapped my arms around his waist, lifting him into the air to toss him sprawling on the bed. Next, I pulled his bed as far from the window as possible and clawed at the noose-like knotted sheet around his neck. All the while Jay said nothing. After I freed his neck I sat down in the middle of the floor with the sheet. It seemed to be my enemy. For fifteen minutes I ripped and shredded it to pieces, breaking most of my fingernails."

The nurse came in. Mrs. Root panted out the story of what had nearly happened, and waited for an answer.

"I thought Mr. Geiger had gone to sleep. . . ."

"He nearly did—permanently," Mrs. Root retorted, advising the lax attendant to seek other employment.

The nurse spun around on his heels, packed, and left the house, driving away in a Cadillac. When he was first hired he came to work in a six-year-old Ford. A check of Geiger's clothes closet showed empty hangers. In the room was a small safe where some of the money clients paid upon coming to the house was kept. It contained only a few hundred dollars—but a fraction of the amount Mrs. Root figured should be there.

Drug reductions continued. Some progress was being recorded in this direction and the grip of the drug was being gradually broken. But pain still wracked his body. He described it as like "living through a daily crucificion at which my tormentors never ran out of fresh spikes."

A month dragged by. It was mid-afternoon and Mrs. Root decided to finish her office work at home so as to be near her husband. When she unlocked the front door, she found a gigantic basket of flowers and a note addressed to her. She read:

Darling:
  It has been a sheer joy living with you—a slice of Heaven: sweet, wonderful, but oh, so very, very short. We had some marvelous times together. Remember: no regrets. I've been too much of a burden to you and this is the only way out. It will be much better for both of us. Kiss the children for me.
                                    I love you,
                                              Jay

As she finished the note she smelled smoke. She knew Rosyln, the maid, had taken Tina to a party, that Mary, another servant, had the day off, and that Bobby was in school—but where was the nurse?

She took the stairs two at a time. A pall of smoke hung over the halls. Her eyes smarted and she coughed as she groped her way toward the master bedroom. Inside, flames were crackling around the shadowy outline of the bed in which Geiger lay unconscious. Guided by instinct and her familiarity with the location of the bed, she reached it blindly, her stinging tears blacking out vision.

Seizing her husband, she dragged him from the room and down the long hallway.

The fire department responded rapidly to her call and the blaze was soon under control. A resuscitator brought Geiger to consciousness.

"Oh, Jay," were the only words Mrs. Root could find when he opened his eyes.

He coughed slightly and whispered, "It would have been better for both of us."

"No, no, no," she cried hysterically.

The missing nurse returned. His face was ashen. "Mr. Geiger said he wouldn't need me for a few hours," he tried to explain. "He wanted me to put some flowers by the front door for someone to pick up. I did this and left. I went to see my mother, who is ill."

"I think," Mrs. Root said coldly, "that from now on you'd better devote full time to your mother."

So another nurse was dismissed.

Six months after the fire, another crisis arose. Home for dinner, Mrs. Root was told by the servants that the nurse had come downstairs to request quiet and for no one to disturb Mr. Geiger, who had finally fallen asleep after a difficult day.

Obeying, Mrs. Root tiptoed about the house and without seeing her husband had dinner in the patio with Tina and Bobby. Midway through the meal Bobby's and Mrs. Root's eyes met. For several seconds they stared at each other.

"What is it, Bobby?"

"I—I just don't know," answered the boy, who was then in high school. "I had a funny feeling."

"Like something is wrong?"

He hesitated. "Yes. . . I think that was it."

Mrs. Root jumped up. "I have the same feeling," she said, starting for the stairs.

When she reached her husband, he was asleep. His color was normal, as was his breathing. She called to him softly. There was no response. She shook him gently; then harder. He slept on.

An empty hypodermic syringe lay on the bed table. She sniffed at it but was unable to tell what it had once contained.

She dialed Dr. Rudner.

"Find the nurse," he commanded. "Find out what he gave Jay. I'll be right over."

She hung up. The male nurse came in, stumbling, intoxicated. Mrs. Root fought to control herself. . . to be an actress. She smiled and casually inquired, "How's the boss tonight?"

"You won't have to worry any more," the nurse answered thickly.

She forced another smile. "Why not?"

"I couldn't stand to see you suffering—a fine, good-looking woman like you—so I fixed everything."

She studied him. "How?" she asked.

"I gave him something," he said mysteriously.

"When?"

"Not long ago."

"What was it?"

The nurse grasped the back of a chair for support. "Just something," he said ambiguously. "Something to knock him out. Permanently." He staggered toward her, his arm encircling her waist. "From now on you won't have to worry," he guaranteed.

She thought of disengaging his arm, then changed her mind

and ventured, "Why don't we go down to the bar and have a drink?"

"Sure, sure."

Downstairs, Mrs. Root slipped behind the polished bar. The nurse seated himself on a stool, leaning on his elbows toward her.

"Bourbon or Scotch?"

"Bourbon," he said.

She poured a stiff drink for him and one for herself. Her hand shook. Thoughts were thronging her mind. Upstairs her husband was dying. . . . Dr. Rudner was coming. . . . Somehow she had to get it out of the nurse what the injection contained.

The nurse raised his glass. "Here's to you," he toasted, adding: "A free woman."

"In how long?"

"Shouldn't be more than an hour. That stuff acts fast."

She raised her glass, allowing the liquor to touch her lips. Bobby, goggle-eyed, was watching from a distance. He knew his mother never drank hard liquor. She set the drink concealingly behind the bar.

"You'd better tell me what was in the injection," she said evenly.

"Don't worry about it," he said, leaning closer to her, his eyes lingering on her face.

She threatened, "It isn't my worry, but it's going to be yours—a great, big worry."

He straightened up. "Why mine?"

"Because there's going to be an autopsy. And the autopsy will show what was absorbed into Mr. Geiger's system."

"What!" he roared, incredibly, his fist pounding the bar. "You want an autopsy!"

"I certainly do and I mean to have one," she said firmly.

"But I—but I. . ."

"You'll go to the gas chamber or, at best, get life," she reminded, "unless. . . ."

"Unless what?" He was thoroughly frightened, spasms of fear penetrating his alcohol-numbed mind.

"Unless you tell me—and I mean tell me immediately," she emphasized, "the name of the drug you gave Mr. Geiger."

He looked at her indecisively.

"Or I'm calling the police," she continued.

His eyes darted about in panic. "Okay, okay," he said, naming the drug and the amount adminstered.

Mrs. Root pointed a finger at him and her voice was steady as she ordered, "Now you get the hell out of here!"

For three hours Dr. Rudner worked over Geiger, finally pulling him back to life. "It was touch and go," he sighed, "and it was lucky I had the name of the drug." He said he would spend the night with the patient and he gave Mrs. Root a sedative.

After four more months of withdrawal, Geiger was off narcotics. He rallied strongly. Mrs. Root was scheduled to try a case before the Supreme Court, and her husband begged to accompany her. Dr. Rudner sanctioned the trip provided a nurse was brought along.

At the conclusion of the case the trio went to New York, registering at the Waldorf. Here Geiger underwent a relapse and was taken to a clinic. Specialists thought the answer lay in the removal of part of his stomach.

They returned to Los Angeles and the operation was performed in the house.

Despite the operation, pain persisted for months. A team of nerve specialists was called into the case. They proposed a short painless operation with a local anaesthetic in a hospital.

"It will be necessary to sever several nerves," they informed Mrs. Root.

"Will he suffer any?" she asked.

They assured her he would not.

One of the lawyer's investigators, Ira Bailey, went with her to the hospital. Extremely loyal, he wished to be around should he be needed. Mrs. Root and Bailey waited outside surgery. A penetrating scream reached their ears.

It was evident that the local anaesthetic wasn't working. Mrs. Root jumped to her feet, begged a nurse to go into the operating room. The nurse said it was against regulations. There were additional screams. Bailey's face became a white mask. Mrs. Root was pacing, her temper rising. At length she burst open the door of the operating room, screaming, "Stop!"

She saw tears streaming from her husband's eyes. She had never known him to cry.

One of the surgeons attempted to placate her. He explained that they had found an infection. She was led from the room. The operation finished, Geiger was loaded into an ambulance, Mrs. Root, Bailey, and the chauffeur trailing it to Hancock Park.

Back at the house, giant blotches suddenly appeared on the chauffeur's face. He was soon to suffer a mental breakdown and be committed to a hospital for the insane.

Ira Bailey made a choking sound and, clutching at his heart, fell to the kitchen floor. This was the first of a series of heart attacks that ultimately claimed his life.

Dr. Rudner, who by now was a close and trusted member of the family, said he would spend the night with Geiger. Insisting Mrs. Root go to bed, he gave her a strong sleeping pill.

"My God," she whispered to him, "what next?"

It was merciful that she could not foretell the future.

Pains and abdominal swelling decelerated recovery. Geiger fretted away the hours in bed, grousing at his inertia. Then one day he proclaimed himself fit, announcing in a voice of authority to his wife that he was going to her office the next day to resume his managing and secretarial duties. He smiled broadly, generating optimism, his spirits apparently buoyed. Mrs. Root could see through the sham, but didn't argue the point and after receiving the sanction of his doctors, permitted him to accompany her to the office.

He tired easily. After three months his labors were reduced to part-time. At the end of another month he tossed in the sponge, admitting in defeat, "I simply can't make it."

They discussed possible hobbies to keep him occupied and he came up with the idea of cooking. This would not be ordinary cooking, but incomparable cuisine that could tempt the most jaded of appetites. He would explore and master the culinary arts, trying his epicurean skills on his wife with the preparation of her favorite dishes. For weeks he studied cooking with wines and learned how to make mouth-watering fancy sauces.

Meals at the house became adventures in eating. So delighted was Geiger at his mastery over gastronomy that his own appetite picked up, until much-needed pounds began to fill out his gaunt frame.

This continued for a year and a half, until an abrupt change developed: he was unable to keep food down for more than thirty minutes. He became too weak to cook any more. His craving for food was insatiable and he would eat as many as ten times each day, only to lose the meal soon afterward.

He was sent to the hospital at the University of California at Los Angeles. After exhaustive tests it was deemed necessary to remove the remainder of his stomach. Six weeks later he returned home, bedridden, with female nurses in attendance. Although the operation had curbed his appetite, his food refused to remain down. Beginning to show signs of failing, he turned to avid spiritual reading.

Mrs. Root had employed a new chauffeur, scarcely bothering, owing to her state of mind, to check his references. Although surly, he seemed a capable driver and she found no fault with him until she made an observation: whenever there was a male passenger he kept sneaking glances at the occupant through the rear-view mirror, his face burning with a strange expression that Mrs. Root failed to understand.

Driving home from Santa Barbara where she had gone to defend—and had won an acquittal for—a client charged with burglary, she discovered to her dismay the meaning of the chauffeur's facial expression. It was pure jealousy.

South of Ventura there was an open stretch of highway. The chauffeur's foot squashed the Cadillac's accelerator until Mrs. Root, leaning forward, saw that the speedometer needle hovered around ninety-five miles per hour.

Alarmed, she called to him to slow up, receiving the odd answer, "I will on one condition."

She asked what it was.

"That you leave your husband."

"Leave my husband," she repeated, thoroughly puzzled. "Why?"

"Because I love you and I want you."

Mrs. Root couldn't believe her ears. The highway took a turn, but the chauffeur didn't slacken the speed. The tires made a whining sound. Mrs. Root braced her feet for what seemed a certain crackup. Surprisingly, the heavy car clung to the ribbon of concrete.

"Please slow down," she pleaded, terrified.

"Life means nothing to me without you," he replied gunning the car even faster. It was a cliché that, uttered under different circumstances, might have been laugh-provoking. Now it sounded deadly.

"But—but. . . ." She groped for words.

"Death for both of us might be better," he said.

She knew her life was in the hands of a dangerous maniac and much depended on her answer.

"I'll consider it," she lied, "just as soon as we get to the house. We'll sit down and talk it over."

Gradually the car slowed to normal speed. Weak and exhausted, Mrs. Root sank back into the seat cushions. The moment she got home, she telephoned the police. Roaring with rage, the chauffeur was dragged away and jailed. After a sanity hearing, he was committed to a mental institution.

Geiger's health steadily deteriorated. Doctors agreed that he must go to a hospital—this time, Mt. Sinai. The patient had something to say on the subject.

"I know I'm going to die," he told his wife. "As long as I know that, I might as well die in my own bed. I love my home and my family. Please let me die right here."

She yielded to his wishes. Bobby, who was now attending the University of Chicago Medical School, made frequent flights to Los Angeles to visit his stepfather. Geiger's illness was having a pronounced effect on Tina. In school the child would break into hysterical crying fits, thinking she might never see her Daddy again. No matter how weak Geiger might be, he'd force his scrawny arms around his daughter, hold her tightly, and tell her to take care of her mother.

He began hemorrhaging. Mrs. Root said, "Jay, I can't stand it any longer. I'm taking you to the hospital where you'll get better care."

She called an ambulance.

"I'm going to die in four days," he said, as the ambulance drove away.

Mrs. Root took his private nurses with him and engaged an adjoining room for herself. On the third night he talked rationally and cheerfully to her. His health rallied and his blood count improved. It was as if a miracle had happened.

"I'm so happy," his wife said to the nurse. "I hope. . . ." Her voice became indistinct.

"What is it, Mrs. Root?" the nurse inquired.

She shook her head; said nothing. But she remembered

something—her husband's prediction. The next day was the fourth day—the day he said he was going to die.

She sat at his bedside throughout the entire fourth day. During the evening she periodically glanced at the clock. It was two minutes before midnight when he began to sing loudly and clearly in a foreign tongue. She recognized the lyrics as German and the tune as a cradle song.

He couldn't speak German.

His singing increased in volume, welling through the hospital room. She rose from her chair and stood alongside the nurse at his bedside. They listened, bodies rigid.

Precisely at twelve o'clock, he died.

Mrs. Root slowly sank to the floor. The nurse helped her struggle to her feet.

"It must have been a song his mother sang to him as a baby," she sobbed. Later she learned it was called "Wiegenlied."

Geiger's body was removed to a mortuary and Mrs. Root went home. One of the first things she did was to look for his pearl ring, wrist watch, and the pearl tie clasp she had given him on his last birthday. He often proudly displayed these presents to visitors. She thought it appropriate that he be buried wearing them.

They were gone.

On October 16, 1958, Jay Geiger was laid to rest in Forest Lawn Cemetery. He was interred in a crypt, wearing his favorite gold-trimmed dinner jacket. Hundreds of floral tributes arrived. For the first time in Mrs. Root's life, flowers —always a source of joy to her—were unable to cheer her.

Medical bills amounted to a hundred and ten thousand dollars, plus some monthly totals of twenty-five hundred dollars for pharmaceuticals.

Life for Mrs. Root and Tina became unbearable in the big house. Memories of Jay haunted every room. To escape, the lawyer and her daughter moved into a suite at the Town

House. Before their departure, an inventory was taken of the household goods. Jewelry, furs, clothing and other items were missing to the tune of between sixty and ninety thousand dollars. Police were called in. Detectives examined the house, theorizing that the thief or thieves had gained entrance by forcing a lock on a basement window.

Mrs. Root and Tina recalled that more than once they had heard or thought they heard strange footsteps in the house and found doors unaccountably open, but dismissed them jokingly as the ghost of the former owner on nocturnal prowls.

At the end of a full year at the Town House, Mrs. Root reopened the Hancock Park house, to discover that memories of her husband had faded only slightly.

"They are still in the house, nearly as strong as ever, and they always will be," she said.

12

CREATURE OF THE NIGHT

Recurrently, Mrs. Root receives warnings from Dr. Rudner. They are unvarying. He'll say, "Slow down, you've got to get some rest."

She tilts her head backward and laughs—a laugh that isn't meant to be transcribed by a writer to paper. She never guffaws, never cackles uproariously. The best she can produce is a tiny chirp of amusement, unspellable but not unmelodic, a musical sound that seems to tinkle deep inside her.

And then Dr. Rudner, knowing his cautions have fallen upon deaf ears, will also laugh, and the masculine hoarseness of his laugh eclipses hers. Then he will shake his head and his face becomes grim.

"I'll try to get to bed early tomorrow night," she'll promise her doctor.

But the tomorrow night never comes; and the next night and the next find the lights still burning brightly in the Hancock Park mansion during what is popularly known as the "wee hours of the morning." For her this phrase is a misnomer. There are no wee hours. Every hour after midnight is a big, important one, crammed with productivity.

It has been sagely said, "There's a time for living and a time for dying," but for Mrs. Root there should be a rider:

"but no time for sleeping." A bed to her is a non-functional piece of furniture that holds her an unwilling prisoner. It is a last retreat when all activity palls. Sleep comes with difficulty. Countless nights she has climbed into her huge canopied bed at four A.M., awakened an hour later and gone down the winding staircase to work on her hobby—an enormous map of the United States standing upright on wooden supports. Here, into the blank outlines of individual states, she glues semi-precious stones simulating the sparking waters of the Great Lakes, the green forests of Oregon, the ruggedness of the Rockies, the aridness of the deserts. . . .

Three years ago a firm publishing law books, Matthew Bender, asked if she was interested in writing a book on the subject of sex in the criminal courts. She thought it a capital idea, telling Jim Chown, her business manager, "It will be restful." In three years she has completed but two chapters. "There just isn't time," she admits.

It is not uncommon to find her personal hairdresser, Douglas Krumwiede, arranging her coiffure in the middle of the night, experimenting with colors that will please a client in the morning. He'll remain with her, working, while a procession of people wishing to retain her services are interviewed. Should a future client call from a jail, she often says to Krumweide, "I'll whip up a batch of fudge first, to give me a second wind," and then she takes off.

Those represented by Mrs. Root seem to make their important moves during the evening. One night she rendezvoused in Beverly Hills with a burglar who, removing his shoes, brought forth thirty-five thousand dollars in diamonds, which he handed her with the words, "Defend me."

At two A.M., many years ago, with her mother as chaperon and a shovel for equipment, Mrs. Root drove to a lonely spot, where she dug up the remains of an infant who had been placed in boiling water. The mystery of the missing corpse needed for evidence was solved.

Four times in the dead of night she left her house to defend a will-o-the-wisp "cat burglar," who, shoeless, broke into houses, taking nothing but a glass of milk and always leaving the same note: "I DID IT AGAIN." Four times Mrs. Root saved him from a jail sentence, but on the fifth offense either the milk was sour or the prowler saw the error of his ways, because he confessed his guilt, throwing himself upon the mercy of the court. Today he is a successful and hard-working probation officer in Los Angeles.

Another night call involved a mortician. Strange noises were detected coming from the workroom where corpses were prepared for burial. The mortician, who had a fetish for fat women, would engage in copulation with any weighty lady brought into the funeral parlor. Arrested, he was charged with rape. Mrs. Root beat the case on the grounds that a corpse isn't a human being.

In a midnight homicide case in which a rich Chinese was beheaded, not a single witness—although many took the stand—would testify against the accused, a client of Mrs. Root's, who was found not guilty. Throughout the trial the same three rows in the courtroom were always filled with Chinese staring hostilely at State witnesses. Seemingly hypnotized by fear, these witnesses leveled no recriminations against the defendant.

After the final verdict a lawyer asked Mrs. Root if she knew the group of Chinese. She shook her head.

The lawyer explained, "They're members of a powerful tong who have threatened war against a rival faction. And isn't it odd," he went on, "that all the witnesses for the prosecution were allied with the rival tong?"

She seemed surprised. "Just a coincidence, I imagine," she concluded.

When the telephone rings and someone needs legal assistance and Mrs. Root dashes off, Douglas Krumweide contends that what sparks her into swift action is decidedly not the promise of juicy legal fees.

"Many of these arrested persons have no funds," he says. "I keep asking myself, 'Why then is she so available?' I believe it's the result of a great mothering instinct and the desire to fight for what seems a hopeless cause. It shows in her eyes—a fire starts burning—when a late night urgency call comes in."

One interesting middle-of-the night call to which Mrs. Root responded was to defend John Rich, a security guard at a defense plant who was facing the serious twin charges of kidnapping and assault with a deadly weapon. The plaintiff was estranged from his wife, Rose Rich, mother of his two children.

Mrs. Rich, a practical nurse, had a long and convincing story to tell. She said that at 10:45 P.M. on March 28, 1960, she got into her car bound for work at the Valley Doctors Hospital in North Hollywood. She had driven about a block and a half when her husband, who had been hiding in the back seat, made his presence known and pointed a gun at her.

She became hysterical and started screaming. He told her to "shut up" and directed her to drive him to his parked car. He then ordered her to get out and into his car. She said, "I won't."

He said, "Rose, don't argue with me. You're on the losing end."

She looked at the gun in his hand and complied with his demands. He started driving. Once when he slowed for a traffic light, she opened the car door to jump but he grabbed her arm, jerking her back into the car, threatening, "Rose, don't try that again or I'll kill you."

Later, he pulled over to the side of the road. He had a rope, which he tied to the arm-rest of the car, across her arms to his side, and tightened it so that she couldn't open the door again. With that, he warned her that he was going to kill her if she tried it again. "You know I'm a marksman, Rose," he threatened.

As they drove along on the outskirts of the city, he told her, "Rose, I'm going to take you to a friend that can talk some sense into you."

They traveled farther and farther, until they were almost in the city of Newhall. He kept looking around, and every time there was any traffic he would stop at the side of the road and turn his headlights out. She said to him, "Well, if you're just taking me to a friend why are you so afraid of being seen or having the car seen at all?"

He just looked at her, answering, "Rose, I'm not taking you to a friend."

He went through Newhall and started up a canyon to a cut-off, coming at last to a ravine, where he turned the headlights out and started down into the abyss. Every few seconds he kept switching the headlights back on to get his bearings as they wound around the steep road.

She was terrified and, because he had the gun, she knew he intended to kill her.

They parked in the ravine all night, until the sun came up. He said, "Rose, I told you that I was going to stop this divorce one way or another and this is the way it's going to be. My life is over with. There's nothing left for me to live for and the children will be better off without you. I'm going to kill myself and you, too. I've written a letter. It will be read to the children."

He went on talking and rehashed all of their marriage. Then she told him, "John, you're too intelligent a man to have those thoughts. Your life isn't over. Far from it. You still have the children."

He replied, "No, Rose, it's too late now. I don't have the children. They've turned against me."

He went on, over and over again, reviewing their past

life together. They talked and he finally said, "You're agreeing with me now."

She had to do this because he was building up to such a dangerous point that to go against him might be worse. She tried to calm him and said at length, "Well, John, I'm tired of fighting you. I can't fight you any more. You've won out."

Finally, he took her home and she called the police.

The case of People of the State of California *vs.* John Rich, from the very onset, moved inexorably against Mrs. Root's client. Despite her efforts five women were chosen on the jury, and Mrs. Root felt she could almost hear their thoughts of . . . "That awful man . . . poor girl . . . abducting a mother of two children at gunpoint."

When the police officers whom Mrs. Rich telephoned were placed on the stand, Mrs. Root questioned them in an almost lethargic manner, causing an out-of-town visitor, expecting legal fireworks, to remark, "What's she got anyway, besides the hat and the clothes?"

He would soon find out. She was like a predatory animal lying in the grass, ready to pounce upon her selected quarry: Mrs. Rich in cross-examination.

She began:

Q. Mrs. Rich, you stated that when you met your husband, the defendant, he was armed with a gun.

A. Yes.

Q. How was he wearing the gun? How did he have the gun in his possession?

A. He had the gun in a holster. A brown holster. Then later, in the ravine, he took the gun and stuck it in his belt.

Q. Was the gun loaded?

A. Yes.

Q. How many bullets were in the gun?

A. Five.

Q. Did you suffer any injuries or bruises from your experiences?

A. No.

Q. When you got in and sat down, the car door on your side wasn't locked, was it?

A. Yes. He reached over and locked it after I tried to escape.

Q. Of course, you knew that the little button could easily unlock it, didn't you? He drove many miles before you claim he tied you to the arm-rest.

PROSECUTOR: I will object to that. That calls for a conclusion of the witness.

MRS. ROOT: I am asking for her knowledge.

THE COURT: Overruled.

A. I didn't intend to run. I knew he had a gun. I wasn't going to run away from him.

Q. During all that time you were parked in the ravine, didn't the defendant ever get out of the car?

A. Yes, to relieve his bladder.

Q. I assume you did also.

A. Yes.

Q. Couldn't you have escaped into the darkness at these times?

A. I was too frightened.

Q. Isn't it a fact, Mrs. Rose, that you engaged in an act of sexual intercourse with the defendant after you parked in the ravine?

A. Well . . . not exactly.

Q. What do you mean, not exactly?

A. He—he forced me into it.

Q. How did he do this?

A. I said to him, I didn't want to have such an act of sexual intercourse with him.

Q. Weren't you kissing the defendant previous to what you say was an act of sexual intercourse?

A. He was kissing me.

Q. What position was the defendant in?

A. I was seated in his lap.

Q. Did you raise yourself up and get on his lap?

A. Not exactly.

Q. If it wasn't exactly, what do you mean by that?

A. I mean to say that I didn't mean to get on his lap.

Q. Did you or did you not get on his lap?

A. (*Sighing*) Yes, I got on his lap.

Q. Isn't it a fact, Mrs. Rich, that the reason you got on his lap was that you had previously engaged in acts of sexual intercourse and it was your usual habit pattern to first sit on his lap before you had the act?

A. Well—well, yes—yes, I did used to do that, but not now because I've been estranged from my husband.

Q. Mrs. Rich, isn't this really what caused the separation, because you told the defendant that you didn't care to sit on his lap any longer because you were in love with another man?

A. Yes, because my husband made me hate him.

Q. So, therefore, because you hated your husband you decided that you had to love another man and you did love another man?

A. Yes.

Q. When you were seated on the defendant's lap, was his lap soft or hard?

A. Why, it was soft.

Q. You didn't feel anything hard about his lap, did you?

A. Not at that time.

Q. When did you feel something hard?

A. Of course when he had an act of sexual intercourse with me.

Q. Is that the only time that you felt anything hard? Think carefully.

A. Yes, it was.

Q. You are sure you weren't sitting on his lap when you felt something hard, were you?

A. No, no, that was when he was having an act of sexual intercourse and he was on top of me.

Q. I wasn't referring to you feeling something hard during the act of intercourse. You previously testified the defendant took the gun from its holster and put it in his belt. Why didn't you feel it?

A. Oh, yes, yes, I forgot. He had taken off the gun and laid it down on the seat.

Q. You couldn't have been afraid of him at that time if it was lying on the seat, because you could have reached over and gotten the gun, couldn't you? It was over close to you.

A. Yes, I guess so, but—but I was too frightened to reach for it.

Q. But isn't it true that you ultimately got the gun? And isn't that how you testified that you knew the gun was loaded because you knew there were five cartridges in the gun?

A. Well, I testified, but—but I guess maybe I made a mistake.

Q. Now Mrs. Rich, you were talking about the fact that you didn't love the defendant anymore because he had made you hate him and you fell in love with another man.

A. Uh . . . yes.

Q. Did you tell the defendant, your husband, about the affairs that you had with this other man?

A. No, no, I didn't ever tell him.

Q. But now think carefully, Mrs. Rich. Didn't you write him a note telling him that he could never be as good or satisfactory sexually as the man you had fallen in love with?

A. No. Oh, no. Decidedly no. I didn't ever tell him that.

Q. Are you quite sure?

A. Why, I certainly didn't do any such thing.

Q. Mrs. Rich, if I would tell you that I have seen a paper allegedly in your handwriting, signed by the pet name that your husband knew you by and the one that he always called you privately, would you admit you write it?

A. I would not. I never wrote such a note.

Q. Your Honor, at this time, I offer this letter for identification. Now Mrs. Rich (*passing her the letter*), will you tell the court and the jury whether or not you have ever seen this document before?

A. Where did you get this?

Q. Have you ever seen it before?

A. It—it certainly looks like my handwriting, but it's a forgery.

Q. What makes you think it's a forgery?

A. Because. . . .

Q. Because what?

A. Because I just don't believe I could have been in my right mind and ever written anything like that.

Q. That is your language isn't it?

A. Yes.

Q. Then wouldn't you say that this really was your note?

A. Well, I guess I was just so jealous at that time and so provoked at him and I wanted to be so important that I wrote this to make him jealous.

Q. Now Mrs. Rich, the defendant didn't really force you into his car at gun-point, did he?

A. Perhaps not.

Q. Please answer yes or no.

A. No.

Q. Actually, you asked him to carry you into the car, for old times' sake, like he had done years ago.

A. Yes.

Q. Before you parted on the morning after being parked in the ravine all night, there was an argument and after you thought it all over you decided to call the police and press charges against the defendant. Isn't that correct?

A. (*Shrugging dejectedly*) Yes, it is true.

The charges against John Rich were reduced to a misdemeanor: carrying a gun (the gun he used on duty at the defense plant) without a licence. He received a six-month suspended sentence and probation.

Mrs. Root received enormous satisfaction and very little in the form of a fee.

The City of Los Angeles has a minor attraction that feebly attempts to compete with San Francisco's unrivaled cable cars, an historic landmark called Angel's Flight. Here, a small tram painted bright orange hauls passengers a short distance up a steep hill to a downtrodden neighborhood of old and dilapidated rooming houses and third-class hotels.

Two Los Angeles police officers testified that around midnight of February 28, 1960, they were summoned to a hotel at the top of Angel's Flight by the manager who complained that three male Mexicans sneaked up the back stairs of the hotel and had entered the bathroom on the fourth floor and locked the door.

Officers kicked the door open. They discovered (or so they later claimed) one of the defendants, Edward Gonzales, with a hypodermic syringe in his hand and the other two men standing next to him. On the toilet seat they observed another hypodermic syringe and spoon with the bottom burned, a bottle cap also having the bottom burned, cotton fibre which appeared to be saturated with blood, four empty capsules containing traces of white powder, and one full capsule filled with white powder, plus numerous matches on the floor.

Police laboratory tests showed the full capsule to contain heroin.

Mrs. Root was retained to defend only one suspect, Edward Gonzales. She concentrated on cross-examination of one of the arresting officers.

Q. Did Edward Gonzales say anything when you burst into the toilet?

A. Yes, he did.

Q. What was that?

A. He stated that the fix was not his and he said, "You didn't catch me with the fix in my hand."

Q. Mr. Officer, did you make an examination of defendant Gonzales?

A. Yes.

Q. What did you find?

A. Nothing on him, only on the floor around him.

Q. Did you use physical force on the defendant at any time?

A. No, I did not.

Q. Did you have any conversation with the defendant, Gonzales?

A. Yes. I asked, is it true that you were just preparing to have a fix? He told me no. I looked in his eyes to see if the pupils were dilated.

Q. Were they dilated in your opinion?

A. No.

Q. Did he show any symptoms, such as attempting to wet his lips?

A. No.

Q. Mr. Officer, after you gained entrance into the toilet what did you do?

A. I immediately put the handcuffs on the men and called for my partner for assistance. Told them not to move.

Q. Did you search them?

A. Yes.

Q. How did you search them?

A. I searched from their heads to their shoes.

Q. Isn't it a fact that you caused their hands to be placed behind them in handcuffs as you were searching them?

A. Yes.

Q. Will you tell the court and jury how it was that the trousers of the defendant, Gonzales, fell off of him?

A. Did what?

Q. Fell off of him.

A. Oh. When he raised his hands up when I had my gun on him and I put on the handcuffs, his trousers fell off.

Q. Did you unhook his trousers in order for that to happen?

A. No, he was thin and the trousers were large for him and when he reached up with his hands his trousers fell off.

Q. Did you see any bruises on the defendant when the trousers fell off?

A. I didn't look.

Q. Is it a fact, Mr. Officer, that at that time you struck the defendant, Gonzales, across the buttocks and across the small of his back with a belt?

A. I didn't do that.

Q. Can you explain to the court and jury how there were stripes on the buttocks and back of the defendant?

A. I don't know unless he hurt himself going out of the room.

Q. Isn't it a fact that the belt of the trousers was on the floor when you left the public toilet?

A. Yes.

Q. And isn't it true that you took the belt off of the trousers?

A. Uh, no, no, the defendant took the belt off himself.

Q. How did he do this?

A. He just reached down and took it off.

Q. But how could he have taken it off when you had his hands behind his back in handcuffs?

A. (*Long pause*) Well, he did that before that happened.

Q. Isn't it a fact that immediately upon your going into the rest room you told him to put his hands behind his back and you quickly snapped the handcuffs onto his wrists?

A. Yes, but I can now remember that before that happened he took the belt out of his trousers.

Mrs. Root placed the defendant, Edward Gonzales, on the witness stand.

Q. Did you have any marks on your body when you left the hotel?

A. Yes.

Q. What were they from?

A. An officer beat me.

Q. With what?

A. My belt.

Mrs. Root: Step down. No further questions.

After short deliberation the jury found Edward Gonzales not guilty. The two co-defendants were not so fortunate. Both are still imprisoned.

In a petty thievery case reminiscent in dollars and sense value of Jean Valjean, who stole a loaf of bread in the Victor Hugo classic, *Les Miserables*, Mrs. Root took up the gauntlet for a German refugee girl accused of stealing a bottle of aspirin. Her name was Gretyl and she had escaped the Gestapo and married a G.I. She was suffering from cancer. Mrs. Root brought her into court carried on a stretcher.

As Gretyl had passed through the check stand of a chain drug store and opened her shopping bag to reveal its contents, the cashier had rung up only the cost of a box of Kleenex, overlooking a bottle of aspirin. In a hurry, Gretyl did not bother to count the change. However, the store manager had seen her take the aspirin and, assuming it was shoplifted, signaled a security guard who followed the girl outside the store and arrested her.

Gretyl, who spoke only broken English, shook with fright. Trying to explain what had happened, she groped helplessly for the correct words. Taken to the store's private office, she was interrogated, accused, searched. It seemed that she was again dealing with the Nazis.

She fainted.

When she revived, a confession was thrust into her hands

and promises made that if she signed it she could go home. Sick, suffering, fear-stricken, she affixed her name to the paper.

Sensing a sympathy-inducing trick, the Attorney for the People objected strenuously to the fact that Gretyl was stretcher-borne into the courtroom, but Mrs. Root was well fortified with sworn medical statements as to her condition.

When Mrs. Root finished questioning the security guard, the jury regarded him as another Eichmann. The coup was administered when she read the confession that Gretyl had allegedly dictated. The English was flawless, syntax perfect.

"Were those her very words?" Mrs. Root asked the security guard.

"Her very words," he confirmed.

Mrs. Root called upon the defendant. She was carried by stretcher and placed at the foot of the witness stand where the bailiff swore her in.

"Now," Mrs. Root said to Gretyl, "tell the court in your own words just what happened."

A torrent of broken English poured from the girl on the stretcher. The court reporter began to perspire and a look of anguish came over his face as his fingers faltered in an attempt to transcribe her statement. It became apparent to the jury that Gretyl's version of our language failed to match the English of the confession.

Mrs. Root received no compensation for gaining an acquittal for her client.

A colleague of hers who happened to drop into the courtroom remarked to her with a disapproving shake of his head, "I don't see what you can get out of a case like this."

She answered, "I got two important things: justice, and rid of a splitting headache."

"I understand the justice part of it," he said, puzzled, "but not the headache."

"I took an aspirin from the evidence," she explained.

Still another time when Mrs. Root dashed off in the middle of the night was for the defense of Robert William Wetzel, accused of murdering a woman, Doris Louise McCarthy, in a downtown Los Angeles hotel. After talking with her client and taking stock of the mounting evidence against him, she said to Wetzel, "Sir, you are in a sorry mess."

Wetzel, a painter by trade, asked, "Is the rope around my neck?"

"There are no ropes or electricity in this State," she corrected him, "but if you take a deep whiff of the future you may get a nostril full of gas."

"I hear none of your clients have ever gone to Death Row," Wetzel said.

"Not yet, but there's always a first time," she reminded.

"I don't want to be number one."

"That will be up to the jury."

Wetzel asked, "What are you going to use for my defense?"

"Medical knowledge."

"Do you have medical knowledge?"

"Not yet, but I'll have it when the trial begins," she guaranteed.

The next week, after a consultation with Dr. Rudner, who recommended certain reading, she purchased eleven medical books, into which she delved nightly. She was well aware that during the trial she was going to tangle with a medical authority, Dr. Don H. Mills, a Los Angeles County Deputy Coroner, and she wished to give a good account of herself.

At a preliminary hearing it was disclosed that at about two o'clock in the morning of June 11, 1960, George Mardell, a room clerk at the La Tosca Hotel, observed Wetzel, accompanied by a woman, register as Mr. and Mrs. Robert Wifel, of San Francisco. It was evident that both had been drinking.

They were taken to room 312, where the defendant asked the clerk to close the window and pull down the shade. The clerk gave the defendant the key to the room and he paid the rental for one night. This key was never returned.

The manager of the La Tosca Hotel, Fred Shannon, came on duty at six-thirty A.M., in relief of the clerk. At about ten or ten-thirty A.M., he saw the defendant leave the hotel alone. Shannon asked him if he had the key and the defendant replied: "No, I'm coming back. I'm in 312."

About an hour and a half later he returned, asking Shannon the check-out time. Informed that it was noon, the defendant said, "If I'm not down by twelve o'clock we're staying over." The manager noted that the defendant had nothing with him when he left the hotel, but that on his return he carried a paper bag containing something that rattled, such as cans or bottles. He also noted that when the defendant left the hotel he had been sober, but when he returned he appeared to have been drinking. This was the last Shannon saw of him.

The next day, June 12th, Shannon reported for work at six-twenty A.M. He noticed that the key to room 312 had not been returned, and that the room rental had not been paid. He then conversed with Stephen Heutter, the houseman, gave him the passkey and told him to check room 312.

This occurred between the hours of ten and eleven A.M. After Heutter had been gone a brief time he called Shannon on the house phone, and asked him to come to room 312. Shannon met Heutter at the door, which he then opened, and saw the victim on the bed. Shannon called the police, who arrived in about twenty minutes.

Detective Sergeant J. H. McCreadie of the Los Angeles Police Department observed the following:

A wastepaper basket at the foot of the bed contained two empty Seven-Up bottles, an empty wine bottle, and an empty whisky bottle; a silk stocking formed the pattern of a noose or stirrup that had been attached to the baseboard of the bed alongside the victim's left leg.

The body of a woman was outstretched on the bed, arms above the head, with the slip and dress torn on the left shoulder; the lower portion of the body was completely exposed; there were blood smears on the clothing and numerous bruises on the arms. Blood also stained the sheets near the face of the victim, which looked as if it had come from hand prints, as though someone had wiped his hands on the sheet.

The victim had hemorrhaged from the nose and mouth. On the inner ankle of the left leg were abrasions about one and a half inches long. Bruises were found on the upper and lower portion of the mouth and on the legs. The nipple of the left breast had what appeared to be teeth marks, with crusted blood around the nipple.

Dr. Mills, after examining the body, expressed the opinion that the victim had died by strangulation. He stated that the injury to the left breast probably had occurred following death. Among numerous other injuries, he found that there was a large tear or laceration in the vagina. He found internal hemorrhages and bruising in the areas of the lymph nodes of the neck and at the base of both sides of the neck. There were hemorrhages around the lobe of the thyroid gland, adjacent to the laryngeal structures and in the ligaments between several of the cartilages of the Adam's apple. There was also a hemorrhage across the base of the tongue.

Based upon the decrease in normal body temperature from the time of death to discovery of the victim, the doctor concluded that death probably occurred sometime between midnight and seven A.M. of June 12, 1960. Detective Sergeant Greeley of the Los Angeles Police Department, the arresting officer, found a bus schedule in the defendant's shirt pocket at the time of arrest. From the defendant's person he removed a paper bearing the name of the victim. Also found in a pocket was a newspaper clipping which related to a case of killing by strangulation, in which the judge was quoted as saying that the killer's term was too light.

The defendant admitted a prior conviction of assault and battery with intent to ravish in Pennsylvania on March 10, 1947.

The odds were stacked high against Mrs. Root's client.

Placing of the defendant on the stand aided his own cause very little. He said he was working at the California Hospital as a painter, and stated that he met the victim in a Main Street bar on Friday, June 10, 1960. They had a few drinks together, did a bit of bar-hopping, and both became intoxicated.

During the course of the somewhat hazy evening, Wetzel claimed he met a man by the name of Kennedy at one of the bars, and that the three of them went to a liquor store where they bought some whisky. They proceeded to Mr. Kennedy's apartment and had a few drinks while the victim shampooed her hair. Then they left the apartment.

Wetzel said that the next thing he remembered was awakening Saturday morning on the street. He testified that he arose, went across the street and had more to drink. He stated that he arrived at the Imperial Hotel about three or four P.M. on Saturday, slept there that night, and awoke about eleven o'clock on Sunday morning.

He had some breakfast and went to an afternoon movie; then had more to drink and returned to his hotel. He stated that he returned before midnight but was indefinite as to the exact hour.

Wetzel had no recollection that he had ever been in room 312 of the La Tosca Hotel or that he had ever signed the register at that hotel. The last time he recalled having seen the victim was Saturday morning at Mr. Kennedy's apartment.

It was established that Wetzel had checked into room 352 of the Imperial Hotel on June 6, 1960. He went to work on

Monday, June 13, but failed to go to work on the following Tuesday, Wednesday and Thursday. He was arrested on Thursday morning when he was at the hospital waiting for his paycheck. At the time of his arrest he failed to tell the officer about the man named Kennedy, or his visit to this person's apartment.

Soon after the trial opened, Dr. Mills was called as a witness by and on behalf of the People. His testimony was voluminous, branching into many technicalities that could have proved difficult for the jury to comprehend. One point, however, none could fail to understand:

PROSECUTOR: Did you form any opinion as to the cause of death of this person you examined?

DR. MILLS: Yes.

PROSECUTOR: What is that opinion?

DR. MILLS: Strangulation.

It was Mrs. Root's turn to question Dr. Mills. The courtroom was only partially filled. The day before, it had been crowded. There was a valid reason for the empty seats, best expressed by a spectator during the noon recess:

"It's all over before it really begins. There isn't any defense. I'll give five to one the verdict's going to be murder in the first degree." He turned to his companions challengingly. "Any takers?"

No takers.

At the counsel table no notes were spread before Mrs. Root. She had been turning over and over in her hand a fountain pen containing red ink. Most of her note-taking and thought-jottings throughout her court appearances were in red ink. She dropped the pen on the table and stood up. Her height was startling, an effect created by a king-sized hat with mammoth red roses which shot high into the air and a blue dress with a drape shape and large white dots.

After a few warming-up cursory questions, the woman

lawyer without wasting time revealed the basis of her defense:

Q. Doctor, what did this woman die of, in your opinion?

A. Strangulation.

Q. Strangulation, and did asphyxia have anything to do with it?

A. Asphyxia is an end result of strangulation.

Q. So that in order to determine for your findings the cause of strangulation, after you determined in your opinion it was strangulation, what do you go to look for—and let's talk in lay people's language.

A. You look for the injuries to the neck, where strangulation usually occurs, first of all.

Q. Now, the injuries to the neck—let's go to the outside of the neck. If you believe that this woman died of strangulation, what would you look for first on the outside of the neck?

A. Any injuries to the skin surface.

Q. Did you look?

A. Oh, yes.

Q. All right. What did you find?

A. I found, as I have described before, the bruise on the under surface of the jaw on the left side, and the two bruises on the left side of the midportion of the neck.

Q. Will you describe those bruises, please?

A. They were described in my report here, if this is what you want me to do, within the left infrandibular region, meaning the chin.

Q. Would you be good enough to tell us . . ."

A. I have told you.

Q. I don't understand you too well. Forgive me for my ignorance.

A. I am sorry.

Q. I want to know, by a bruise, how long was it? Was there a cutting of the skin? What did it look like?

A. The bruise, of course, involves only discoloration of the skin caused by hemorrhage within that region. There was no cutting of the skin.

Q. No tears?

A. No tears.

Q. No blood, as far as you saw?

A. Not on the external skin surface.

Q. We are talking about the external surface?

A. Yes.

Q. Any breaking of the skin at all?

A. No breaking of the skin at all.

Q. So, then, it can be said that your findings as far as the bruise was concerned was a reddened or discolored mark upon the skin—is that correct?

A. Yes.

Q. Did they look like finger marks to you?

A. This is something I could not say.

Q. Did they look like something that was tied tight around the neck to you?

A. No.

Q. Did you form an opinion as to what caused those bruises?

A. Only to the extent of the injury.

Q. On the outside, I am talking about.

A. That's correct.

Q. What was your belief in that regard?

A. They could be caused by any force causing injury to the cutaneous skin surfaces.

Q. Isn't it a fact that when force is used in order to cause strangulation, Doctor, we usually find the fingerprints, if that force is used?

A. Not necessarily. No.

Q. Well, fingerprints are left under such circumstances, aren't they?

A. It has happened.

Q. And you could really tell they were fingerprints?

A. In many cases, yes.

At recess time Mrs. Root lunched with Eugene V. Mc-Pherson, a capable attorney connected with her office. She asked him how he thought it was going.

"Very well," he replied.

She pressed him for further comment, inquiring, "How do I sound with all my newly-acquired medical folderol?"

"You sound both highly competent and terribly naive," McPherson answered. "Sort of—" He paused searching for an example, and when it came to mind said: "Like a doctor who just performed a miraculously successful operation and when the patient came out of the anaesthetic asks him, 'Do you think I stitched you correctly?'"

"Good," Mrs. Root nodded. "That's the way I tried to sound."

Mrs. Root bathed and changed her entire wardrobe in her office dressing room. Upon her arrival at superior court every seat was filled. Word had circulated that the clothes horse of the courtrooms was sharpening her defensive weapons.

The cross-examination continued:

Q. Now, then, on the internal side of the neck, you found hemorrhages. Is that correct?

A. Yes.

Q. And those hemorrhages were found specifically where?

A. On both sides of the neck within the subcutaneous tissues, and also within the muscular tissues on both sides of the neck as well as around the lobe of the thyroid gland and adjacent to the laryngeal structures, the Adam's apple, and also in the ligaments between several of the cartilages of the Adam's apple.

Q. In connection with those hemorrhages, you found no fractures?

A. Correct.

Q. You found nothing broken within the inside of the neck?

A. That's right.

Q. You found nothing torn on the inside of the neck, did you?

A. That's correct.

Q. In fact, you found, as far as the muscles and tissues and whatever bone structure that there is, if there is any, you found all of that intact, didn't you?

A. Yes, except for the hemorrhages described.

Q. And hemorrhages are caused by what, please?

A. Bleeding.

Q. Anything else?

A. Injury.

Q. Injury. Such as?

A. Any type of blow, pressure, ligatures—any of pressure or blow.

Q. If you found any blow, you would have found it externally, wouldn't you?

A. Not at all.

Q. Did you ever see a strangulation case where there was a traumatic force used externally that you didn't find some fracture?

A. Oh, yes.

Q. Is that quite common?

A. When you say common, do you mean does it happen in more than fifteen percent of the cases?

Q. That would be my understanding.

A. I would say probably not. It is not common to that extent.

Q. Do you ever find where traumatic force has been used causing strangulation that there isn't some bruise left externally or some marking externally from the force?

A. Yes, I have found that.

Q. Is that common?

A. Not common.

Q. How much would be the percentage of the chances of some findings?

A. I don't think I could give you a percentage except that it's less than fifty.

Q. As to the matter of hemorrhaging. If a person was an alcoholic and under the influence of liquor to the extent of .27 as you previously testified, have you ever known of such a person dying of asphyxia caused from an alcoholic condition?

A. I have never seen one. I have read of it.

Q. In fact, medically speaking, it is known to be a cause of asphyxia. Isn't it?

A. Well, now, you are leaving out some of the intermediate parts.

Q. Maybe you'll, with your professional help, assist us?

A. If we are thinking about the same thing, we are assuming some type of blow to the neck. It is well known that alcoholics are more susceptible to asphyxial deaths from some type of neck injury, particularly those injuries over the carotid body in which there would be a reflex death or stoppage of the heart. This is not asphyxial death, but it is a death due to injury in the neck in a alcoholic.

Q. Let's assume that a person is love-making and a person in that love-making is either being kissed or hugged about the neck—there is excitement sexually; she is an alcoholic as you have found this woman to be at the time, and one whose liver condition was in the condition that hers was in. Would you find such a situation as asphyxia?

A. It could happen, but I'd say again it's not asphyxia. It's a reflex type of death from pressure on the carotid body.

Q. And when you say pressure, you mean that such as as love-making wherein some external force such as a person hugging or pressing in some fashion or kissing or something of that sort can be such pressure?

A. Yes.

Q. You found a condition of the liver in the deceased, and you said that the liver weighed more than the usual.

A. That's true.

Q. It is a liver condition you find in alcoholics, is that correct?

A. Many alcoholics, yes.

Q. Doctor Mills, what is the content of alcohol in the blood stream which causes one to be intoxicated?

A. For driving purposes, it is recognized that .15 percent of alcohol in the blood stream makes most people too intoxicated to drive.

Q. You found no residue of foods, or anything of that sort, in the stomach of the victim?

A. No.

Q. About how long is it that food remains in the stomach so that we would reasonably be expected to find it?

A. That all depends on how much is taken in, what the condition of the body is—that is, if you were to take in some food, it would probably be out of the stomach within a period of four to six hours.

Q. So you could reasonably conclude that there hadn't been any food during four to six hours previous to death?

A. I think that's fair.

Q. Is it true, or isn't it true, that alcohol has a greater effect upon a person whose stomach does not have any food in it than if there was food there?

A. This goes to the effect of how quickly it is assimilated to the stomach. If there is nothing else to dilute the alchohol or compete with the assimilation, yes, it would go into the blood stream at a quicker pace.

Q. Now, Doctor, as to the arms, did you find any injury at all upon the arms of Mrs. McCarthy externally?

A. No, no recent injuries.

Q. So that if there had been anything holding the arms down, such as a stocking, you would have probably been able to have found some indication on the outside of the skin, wouldn't you have?

A. Not necessarily.

Q. But you possibly. . . ."

A. Oh, possibly, yes.

Mrs. Root called two witnesses for the defense—John Oppenheimer and James Walter Longworth—who testified that they were residents of the Hotel La Tosca during the dates in question, residing in rooms near the room in which the body of Mrs. Doris McCarthy was found; that at no time during their residence there, and particularly during the days in question, did they hear any unusual noises, commotion, or any sounds suggesting movement emanating from room 312. They further stated that they heard no screaming or movement of furniture or anything that aroused their suspicions or gave them reason to recall the possibility of a struggle or any foul play.

Also called to the stand as a witness for the defense was Lola Torres, manager of the Rangeley Apartments, who said she knew the deceased under the name of Mrs. Lee Wood and that she lived for three years, on and off, at that apartment building.

Among the relevent questions asked her and the answers received were the following:

Q. Did you ever see Doris McCarthy intoxicated?

A. Yes, many times.

Q. What do you mean by many times?

A. Well,—if a person lies in your hallway dead drunk, she should be drunk.

Q. I don't understand. Could you explain that?

A. Well, she'd be lying there in the hallway with her purse open and her shoes off and just snoring away.

Q. Would you smell liquor on her breath?

A. Yes.

Q. Did you sometimes see her drink?

A. Yes, many times.

Q. How many times?

A. Every day, practically. The many times I saw her—I never saw her sober.

Q. Did you receive a complaint in 1959 from Doris McCarthy as to whether or not she had liver trouble?

A. Yes.

Q. When was that?

A. Right about—about the latter part of '59. She was saying that she had to go to the hospital. She dreaded it because she knew it was a liver ailment, and I told her her stomach was so bloated.

Q. Did you ever see the police come and get her?

A. Well, could I describe that the way. . . .

PROSECUTOR: Your Honor, I'll stipulate that the lady was arrested on many occasions. I think it's immaterial, specifically for this witness to testify to it. I don't know what bearing it has on this case. It's immaterial.

MRS. ROOT: If Your Honor pleases, if counsel is agreeing that she has a long arrest record—you have the arrest record, don't you, Mr. Mayer?

PROSECUTOR: I stipulate, Your Honor, that she has been arrested on many occasions, for resorting and for drunkenness. There are records here. The records are here, Your Honor.

THE COURT: Does the defense accept the stipulation?

MRS. ROOT: Yes.

Q. Now Mrs. Torres, calling your attention to the time that she was residing there, did you ever see Doris McCarthy in the rooms with men not her husband?

A. Yes.

Q. At any time in the year of 1959 or '58, when you saw Doris McCarthy passed out, did you ever hear her scream?

A. Well, just once I had to get up because she was screaming practically by my door. We had a vacant couch outside, and she was screaming, "Murder, murder," because there was a guy there, and they were drinking, and she was screaming, "Help, help," so I went out there and wanted to know what she wanted.

Mrs. Root called Jack Feld as a witness for the defense. Feld, a café owner, said he knew the deceased for about six or seven years and had seen her quite often during that period at his place; and that on numerous occasions he had observed that she was intoxicated and had refused to serve her.

The criminal record of Doris McCarthy was read to the court and jury indicating numerous arrests for offering, resorting, and intoxication.

For her summation, Mrs. Root did not have to reload her legal weapons with fresh ammunition. She had already fired her blasts with telling effect, and it was now only a matter of refreshing the minds of the jurors where the shots had struck home.

In essence, she told the jury:

"This case is one of circumstantial evidence. No unusual noises were heard during the dates in question by neighbors in the immediate vicinity and there was no evidence of a struggle of any kind. There were no blood stains or smears anywhere else in the room except in the bed area, clothing, bedding and body.

"The deceased, Doris Louise McCarthy, was a chronic alcoholic and was suffering from a liver ailment apparently due in part to her excessive drinking. It was also shown that the deceased had an extensive arrest history for intoxication and resorting.

"The Coroner who performed the autopsy testified that he found numerous external and internal injuries to the body, including lacerations, abrasions, bruises and hemorrhages. He stated that there was severe injury both externally and internally to the vaginal region, but did not ascribe death to these injuries. On the contrary, he reported that these injuries and others could have been incurred after death, thereby eliminating them as the cause of death. He related the death to manual strangulation caused by some force, blow, or pressure to the neck area.

"It is the opinion of the attorney for the defendant that because there is no evidence of any criminal act having been committed against the deceased which can be relied upon as the cause of death, that the prosecution has failed to establish the corpus delicti.*

"Although it is true that the corpus delicti can be proved by circumstantial evidence, there must be evidence from which it can reasonably be inferred that the external force or violence causing the death was applied by another and was not self-inflicted or the result of an accident. The prosecution at no time established the death of the deceased as causally related to a criminal agency.

"At no time throughout the entire record is there ever an opinion ventured as to what caused the discoloration marks noted on the deceased's neck. There is neither proof that the discoloration was caused by some type of cloth, nor that it was caused by finger marks. However, it was stated by the Coroner that strangulation resulting from pressure applied by hands can and does leave identifiable prints. This was not the case here. The doctor testified on cross-examination that more likely than not in an instance where traumatic force is exerted, causing strangulation, finger marks would be present.

"The Coroner testified that the deceased was intoxicated prior to death and that findings also indicated an abnormal liver condition usually related to alcoholism. He also stated that it is well known that alcoholics are more susceptible to asphyxial deaths from some type of neck injury, particu-

* The basic facts necessary to the commission of a crime, as, in murder, the actual death of the person alleged to have been murdered— often used erroneously to designate the body of the victim.

larly those injuries over the carotid body in which there would be a reflex death or stoppage of the heart.

"He also admitted that pressure arising out of sexual excitement or love-making, wherein there was evidence of hugging, could constitute the kind of pressure or force relating to the injury of the deceased."

It was after this latter innuendo that Mrs. Root paused and took a few swallows of water before continuing:

"It is contended that since there was no evidence presented as to the manner by which the pressure, force, or blow could have occurred which the prosecution alludes to as the cause of death, that the only rational conclusion would be the correct assumption in light of the evidence presented, that either the deceased, while suffering from a liver ailment and in an intoxicated state, grabbed her own throat while having spasms in her throat and thereby exerted the pressure referred to as the cause of death, inflicting upon herself the fatal wound.

"An equally compatible theory would be that while the defendant and the deceased were in the throes of making love—a violent experience at best—accidental excessive pressure was exerted which caused the hemorrhages as found. It is known from the autopsy that the deceased was drunk prior to death, and it can be inferred from testimony that she was seen to be drunk, further borne out by the empty liquor bottles present in the room.

"Certainly, one of the elements of the corpus delicti has incontrovertably been established, that is, the death of a human being. Further, it is urged that though fortune did not smile at the deceased but rather found her ill, wanting, and in undesirable position, nonethless she was a human being and her life was as precious to her as anyone's.

"Well, ladies and gentlemen of the jury, the life of Robert William Wetzel is also precious to its owner—far too precious to take away on circumstantial evidence. I leave the decision in your hands."

The jury returned a verdict of manslaughter, which automatically carries a one to ten year sentence.

Mrs. Root returned to her Hancock Park home, undressed slowly, and luxuriated in a bathtub filled with warm water. Within easy reach was a freshly opened box of chocolates. Four of the confections were already missing.

Downstairs one of the servants remarked to another, "I don't believe I've ever Mrs. Root so completely relaxed."

While Mrs. Root's body, immersed in the soothing water, might have been relaxed, her mind was spinning swiftly to prepare the defense of a stripteaser known as "The Leopard Woman," who had been arrested by vice squad officers and charged with a lewd exhibition.

As she chewed on her sixth piece of candy, this one having a nut fudge center, she believed she had her answers.

13

SLOW BOAT TO PANAMA

If, during the heat of the summer of 1961, a book-maker could have been found who quoted prices on human lives, the odds on the outcome of the trial of the State of California *vs.* John Wesley Riley might have soared as high as twenty-five to one for execution of the defendant. Certainly they wouldn't have dropped lower than nine to one, because that was the number of witnesses who testified they saw Riley shoot his estranged wife, Margie.

All the principals in the trial—a long, costly one to the taxpayers—were Negroes.

What began as a conventional killing, with the State demanding the death penalty, slowly ascended the ladder of sensationalism until it captured the fancy of the Los Angeles newspapers, both white and Negro. Perceptive court reporters should have sensed from the outset that it was to be no ordinary trial. The tipoff was contained in the identical sentence they wrote:

"Riley is represented by Atty. Gladys Towles Root, who claims her client is innocent."

Mrs. Root entered a plea for her client of not guilty and not guilty by reason of insanity. Riley, 42, a cab driver, had been separated from his wife of the same age for seven months. Riley charged that his wife, a former choir singer at the Progressive Baptist Church, had deserted him shortly after a new choir master, Andrian Hartnet, started teaching there.

"Instead of choir singing, he must have had a sideline of love songs," Riley speculated.

Riley reportedly believed his wife had left town, but discovered that she was still there and still seeing Hartnet, although both had long since severed their connection with the church.

From the very beginning, evidence began piling up against Mrs. Root's client. The State scored heavily and decisively with each new witness. In Riley's behalf a handful of friends paid compliments to his character, attesting to his fine church record.

Riley took the stand in his own defense. If he were allowed to tell his incredible story, there was, Mrs. Root believed, a chance to save his life. But there was sure to be an objection. Should the objection be sustained, the remainder of the trial would be a mere formality for the doomed defendant.

Riley claimed that both Hartnet and Mrs. Riley had threatened to put a hex on him and had made mention of poison. He also contended that a minister warned him not to accept food or drugs from his wife or Hartnet because they practiced voodoo and were going to use it to keep him away.

At this juncture, Deputy District Attorney John Galliano leaped to his feet, objecting to the introduction of voodoo allegations. Superior Court Judge Frederick W. Mahl cleared his throat. It was an important decision for Riley.

Judge Mahl ruled that he would accept the testimony because he felt that it would help to show the frame of mind Riley was in the day he went to his wife's residence with a gun in his hand. In view of Riley's long and active service in the church, the judge said he felt this was important.

Riley said that to counter the curse that was surrounding

him he turned to voodooism. He called a high priest to his home and gave him some of the clothes his wife had left behind when she separated from him.

The priest then put his arts into practice. He sprinkled the clothes with powerful powders. He mumbled incantations. He wafted some of the powders through the air. The rites lasted for three days. Then the priest and Riley buried the clothes under the ground.

As Mrs. Root later pointed out to the jury, Riley believed that these other-world influences would counteract the evil spell Mrs. Riley had cast on him and would eventually bring them together.

He had high hopes as he went to see his wife, but her attitude destroyed them immediately. He claimed she heaped abuse upon him, threatened him, and withdrew. He promptly called in another voodoo artist, a priestess, confident that all he needed were stronger powers to overcome his wife's black magic. At the direction of the priestess, Riley sprinkled salt on his wife's shoes and buried them; he put a special oil in his bath; he muttered magic words.

Evidence of his wife's voodoo directed against him, Riley stated, was proved by the finding of two of her dresses covered with special powder in the back yard of his home.

Mrs. Root asked him the following questions:

Q. How was your health during the time you were being hexed?

A. I couldn't eat, lost weight, couldn't sleep, developed ulcers, and I needed medication for my nerves.

Q. Anything else?

A. Yes. The skin began peeling off my hands.

Q. What did the priestess tell you to do?

A. She said to get a gun. That my life was in danger. That whenever I saw my wife to hold the gun close to protect myself. She said to go to see her and it was my last chance or I would lose my life.

Shortly therafter, the defendant claimed, he became so unnerved that he began to drink. It was while he was in such a highly nervous state that he swallowed a voodoo drug. A spirit manifested itself, assuring him that his wife would come back to him if he again would go to her house. He obeyed and related that when he arrived at his wife's address —the home of a cousin—she came out and began to scream and curse and call him names. He thought she had a gun.

He had his own gun, which he took out and shot wildly. His wife fell to the ground, and he got into his car and drove away. An hour later he walked into the Newton Street Police Station and told the sergeant:

"If you found my wife shot, I must have done it."

Then he collapsed, remaining in a stupor that night and the next day.

The prosecution concentrated on corroborated statements of witnesses—nine in all—who said Riley had chased his wife a hundred and fifty-eight yards, cornered her against a fence before their horrified eyes and—while her back was turned and she had dropped to her knees begging for mercy and forgiveness—shot her in the head and back.

In her remarks to the jury Mrs. Root stressed the powers that voodoo can exert and their influences on believers. "John Wesley Riley," she said, "is the victim of a compelling belief in the supernatural powers of the evil eye, the hex and the occult and sinister devices of voodooism. It was an unconscious act that was controlling him and therefore not malice aforethought," she summed up.

Riley was adjudged sane at the time the act was committed, found guilty, and sentenced to life imprisonment. He had beaten astronomical odds by avoiding a death sentence.

Mrs. Root had worked hard on the Riley case, mostly at night behind the purple-painted glass doors of her downtown office. At its conclusion she announced, "I'm going to take a holiday."

"Where?" asked her business manager.

"Las Vegas."

"Why Las Vegas?"

She replied, "Because you can't relax there. Relaxation would kill me."

At the Nevada resort she met an old friend, a cattle rancher who had come to try his luck at the gaming tables.

"Going to do any gambling, Gladys?" he asked her.

She smiled. "I gamble every day with human lives. For me to gamble for merely money would seem pretty hollow."

He shrugged. "To each his own," and then he asked a hypothetical question: "Tell me, if you did gamble—say at roulette—what would you play?"

Her mind was still on John Wesley Riley. She remembered the anguished eyes set deeply in their dark-skinned background, and had a sudden hunch.

"I'd play the black," she said, "and let it ride."

The rancher disappeared in the crowd. He returned in twenty minutes carrying his Stetson hat upside down in both hands. It was brimming over with chips.

His flushed face twisted into a happy grin as he spied Mrs. Root and said, "I took your advice. Black came up seven times in a row. I made a hatful."

"So I see," Mrs. Root replied. She didn't seem surprised.

Back in Los Angeles, Mrs. Root resumed practice. She achieved a victory skein of nineteen consecutive acquittals for clients. Her record was so impressive that it inspired the Bard of Skid Row to compose another verse just before he tilted his head backward to drain a wine bottle:

> "Root-de-toot, root-de-toot,
> Here's to Gladys Towles Root.
> I'm here to do repentance
> She got me a suspended sentence."

"I'm lucky," Mrs. Root told a reporter, elaborating: "Many persons are forced to move to where there is the greatest number of opportunities in their chosen business or profession. I was born in a city that ranks third in the nation's crime standings. Only Reno and Las Vegas lead us."

The reporter asked, "May I quote you on that?"

"No, but you may quote J. Edgar Hoover," she said.

"May I ask you a few questions?"

Mrs. Root nodded.

"Where is crime rising fastest?"

"In cities of 500,000 to one million people.

"What particular type of crime is increasing fastest?"

"Probably bank robberies. They've almost tripled in six years."

The reporter next asked, "What about embezzlements?"

"They've nearly doubled in the last eight years."

"And assaults?"

She thought a moment. "I can't quote exact percentages, but there are more and more every year."

Mrs. Root consulted her wrist watch, an indication that the interview was over. The reporter thanked her. As they parted, she asked him, "Do you own an automobile?"

"Sure," he said. "Why?"

"Better keep an eye on it then," she warned. "An automobile is stolen in this country every 1.5 minutes of each day and night."

Two cases involving charges of murder came her way. One concerned a woman who had operated a facial rejuvenation business for sixteen years. The possessor of a pharmaceutical license, Mary Penny, 59, beauty expert, asserted she practiced no plastic surgery; she merely tightened the facial muscles.

While under her care in the midst of a treatment, a patient died. Mrs. Root, in Mary Penny's defense, proved that the dead woman not only was suffering from ill health but was exceptionally weak from a crash dieting program.

Her client was convicted of involuntary manslaughter. She was ordered to refrain from engaging in such work without obtaining the proper license, and to make restitution to the family of Mrs. Kay Stanley, the deceased.

At Vacaville, a prison twenty miles from Sacramento, there was a stabbing and an inmate died from knife wounds in the abdomen. The defendant asked for Mrs. Root. She traveled there with Jim Chown, who acted as photographer, taking shots of the corridor where the knifing occurred.

"I want to plead guilty," the suspect told Mrs. Root.

"You'll do no such thing," she snapped. "Guilty is a word that I forbid you to even think of, let alone use."

He was freed of the charges.

Jim Chown is a kindly, soft-spoken man. His position of business manager finds him riding a stormy sea of activity in the eye of a hurricane to weather the many daily crises bursting upon the office. While his duties with the Root organization are supposedly confined to purely business, they exceed these boundaries. He tries to keep a watchful eye on his employer, much as a mother would over an errant child. This is not easy. He is dealing with a woman who could tax the physical endurance of a company of battle-hardened marines.

On weekends when some grab tennis rackets and others sprawl in comfortable chairs to erase memories of the working week just concluded, Mrs. Root is on her way to Atascadero, Vacaville, San Quentin, Folsom, Tehachapi, to mention some of the prisons where she discusses the progress of clients who have lost cases or been sent to these corrective institutions for periods of observation and therapy before being returned to private life.

On these trips Chown is behind the wheel of the car and Mrs. Root rides in the rear seat, totally oblivious to scenery or road hazards. She is a woman devoid of physical fear, with one exception: insects. A bug buzzing around her head can cause her genuine alarm.

She had just lowered the car window, as they sped through the flatness of the San Joaquin Valley, to shoo a small insect out into the dry heat, when she remarked, "Jim —do you know what I hate about bugs?"

"No, what is it?" Chown inquired in his soft voice.

"It isn't their size or looks or color," she began. "I think it's because if they bite me I can't retaliate except to kill. And I don't believe in an-eye-for-an-eye. A bug can commit an act inflicting pain and if it's fast enough, get away with it. A bug can't be brought into court. A bug is outside the realm of law. I don't like that."

By nature, Chown is a perfectionist, a slide-rule thinker who moves slowly but carefully and in the right direction. When it comes to Mrs. Root, he is a worrier. An example was the day air conditioning was installed in the offices. It worked perfectly, with the exception of her private bathroom. He knew of her love for a bath between courtroom appearances. At the close of the working day he stayed in the office, donning a pair of coveralls. He remained until four A.M. When he left a smile of satisfaction covered his tired face: the bathroom air conditioner was functioning.

Sometimes Chown is overprotective toward Mrs. Root. It is her health that is, to him, of cardinal importance. He understands men and women and machines. But not Mrs. Root. To him her energy is an enigma.

He has tried futilely to slow her down. Three years ago, after doctors and other advisers had failed, he gained his greatest triumph. He talked her into a pleasure trip; not by car or private plane, but by—of all unbelievable (for Mrs.

Root) means of transportation—a slow Norwegian freighter bound for Panama. Chown, along with Mrs. Root's daughter Christina, would accompany her.

"There's nothing to do but sit and relax all day and night," Chown pointed out, adding as a sales clincher, "and not an insect within miles."

"I'm sold," she said.

"And furthermore," Chown continued, "we'll be at sea over Christmas, which means you'll escape a house full of people and all your preparations."

The *Risanger* was berthed at Long Beach and the arrival of Mrs. Root and entourage brought the Scandinavian crew to the railings. Suitcase after suitcase went up the gangplank.

One of the seamen, eyes popping, cracked, "I'd have washed my dungarees if I'd known royalty was coming aboard."

"They don't have royalty in the United States," corrected another.

"I don't know about that," the seaman said doubtfully, his eyes fixed on the hat and the glittering sequins on Mrs. Root's dress, "she sure looks like a queen in all those clothes."

It proved a friendly, informal, casual sort of voyage on an immaculate ship. Mrs. Root suffered no seasickness. She had only one skirmish with the ocean, when she inadvertently left a porthole in her cabin open and part of a high wave tried to go to bed with her.

Two days before Christmas, Mrs. Root began unpacking some of her luggage. The contents revealed presents for the captain and crew, and decorations. By Christmas Eve she had transformed the *Risanger* into a veritable floating forest, complete with a decorated tree, trimmed tables and bedecked cabins.

It was a Christmas celebration long to be remembered by the officers and crew. On the open deck of the five-hundred-foot-long vessel the crew—abetted by Mrs. Root in her wide skirt whirling arm in arm with the captain—performed their traditional Norwegian dances around the tree. Mrs. Root wore a flaming-red knit dress covered with several hundred ermine tails.

Only the officers spoke English. Mrs. Root taught the sailors to sing "Jingle Bells" and the lyrics came out: "Yingle Bells, Yingle Bells . . . yingle all the vay."

Captain Wold invited Mrs. Root and party to sail through the Panama Canal as his special guests. A table laden with hors d'oeuvres and drinks was set up and the captain explained the various locks and processes enabling ships to travel from one ocean to another. Friends of Chown met them when they debarked, driving them to Panama City, where the visitors were entertained by the President and the Governor.

Subsequently, whenever the *Risanger* docks at Long Beach, Captain Wold and some of his officers are picked up by Mrs. Root's car and brought to the Muirfield Road house for dinner and afterwards returned to their ship.

Captain Wold commented, "After every trip the passengers always say, 'You must stop and see us next time you're in port,' but it never goes any farther than that. Mrs. Root sincerely meant her invitation, and it was the first time in my thirty years at sea that anyone followed through and was so accommodating."

A picture of Mrs. Root and a four-column story appeared in the Panama City newspaper. A few excerpts follow:

> Panama's visitor is spectacular. She is an individualist. She likes what she wears, and she wears what she likes, without undue regard for conventionalism. The rule applied to the courtroom, living room, street and office. She condemns American women for their "sheep-like attitude" toward clothes.
>
> Four trunks filled with stunning garb accompanied her on the voyage. Her fondness for draped fabric is apparent in a

rose print creation. She has added a truly individual accent to a luxurious black satin dress and coat ensemble, on which she has handpainted a galaxy of flowers in her favored warm tones of yellows, oranges, chartreuse and cerise.

Guests in her suite at the Panama Hilton were received by a hostess clad in a unique costume of fused violet, bordered with silver rickrack and fringe. For a reception given in her honor by Mr. and Mrs. C. O. Perkins, she chose a sleek draped sheath of 24-carat gold jersey.

She and her party plan to return to Los Angeles Wednesday. Two days later, armed with the familiar yellow legal pad, she will enter the courtroom on behalf of a man accused of trying to murder his wife and mother-in-law.

For Gladys Towles Root it will be a familiar role. She has served as counsel for the defense in courts of several states, as well as the U.S. Supreme Court. But for her, every case is a new and different story, each defendant a human being who is entitled to his day in court under democratic justice.

After a two-and-one-half week stay in Panama the travelers enplaned for Guatemala. After two days of sightseeing they boarded another plane for Los Angeles.

A few hours out of Guatemala, Mrs. Root was conversing with a fellow passenger from San Francisco when a wandering thought came to Christina. Breaking into the conversation, she asked, "Mother, have you ever been in the Tehachapi Women's Prison?"

"Oh, why certainly, dear," Mrs. Root answered. "I've been in and out of there a dozen times."

The passenger paled and excused himself.

"Did I say something wrong?" Christine questioned.

"No," her mother replied, "but I believe I did. The poor chap must have thought I was Ma Barker."

14

CLOUDY OR CLEAR

Neither rain nor sleet nor snow nor gloom of night could stay Gladys Root from her appointed rounds. But on July 15, 1963, something did.

Measles.

Red blotches just below her neck made their conspicuous debut during a lawsuit for recovery of property in excess of fifteen million dollars. For forty-eight hours prior to the discovery the lawyer had felt queasy, yet the warning signs of the malady had gone unheeded, failing to interfere with her customary sixteen-hour daily working schedule.

It was Judge Stephen S. Weisman in Department 27, Superior Court, who first noticed that the star performer in his courtroom was not up to par. He whispered to the bailiff, who poured a glass of water and carried it to the counsel table. Mrs. Root took one hasty swallow and rushed from the room.

The Judge declared a recess.

Jim Chown drove her to the office of Dr. Rudner, who diagnosed, "You have the measles."

"Is that all?" she said, annoyed.

He nodded.

"What kind of measles, Doctor?"

He told her, "What you have is called three-to-five-day measles," adding: "and knowing you as I do, it's pretty safe to assume they'll last only three days."

"What do I do now?"

"You go home and get into bed."

She gasped, "In the middle of the afternoon?"

"Yes, in the middle of the afternoon," he repeated sternly and gave her some medication.

When the lawyer left the doctor turned toward his nurse, sighing, "There goes one woman you can count on for full disobedience of a doctor's orders."

She rode home in silence. This untimely illness was going to shatter her plans for tomorrow. Her itinerary called for her to fly to Sacramento, rent a car and chauffeur, and be at Folsom Prison by noon, to confer with two clients who were doing time for murder and a morals charge. Then on to Tracy, a correctional institution connected with the Youth and Adult Authority, and to Vacaville and San Jose to discuss a pending trial with relatives of her client.

She was, she thought morosely, going to have to revamp her schedule. But to stay in bed—never.

As she sat in the rear seat of the car, knitting and purling at a furious pace, her mind drifted to a résumé of the week just concluded. It hadn't lacked variety. She had started off the week in a high-spirited mood, given a stratospheric lift by wearing a daring low-necked creation which she and her dressmaker had dreamed up in the middle of the night.

When the judge entered the courtroom and took his seat on the bench his gaze anchored itself on Mrs. Root. His eyes widened. His eye brows arched toward his hairline. Motioning to the bailiff, he scribbled on a piece of note paper and handed it to him. Clearing his throat, the bailiff announced to the court in general:

"We will recess for a short period of time to allow any person present whose body is overly exposed to make certain alterations that will eliminate a nudity which now prevails."

At the finish of the recitation the courtroom emptied. Though no one was singled out, there wasn't a person present who doubted that Mrs. Root was the target of His Honor's disapproval.

If the judge had expected Mrs. Root to rush to her office and reappear in a different dress, he was doomed to disappointment. When court reconvened, she was clad in the same outfit, but now what seemed to be scalloped lace covered her neck and upper bosom.

The judge blew on his glasses and cleaned them carefully with a pocket handkerchief. Then he glanced sharply at Mrs. Root. Apparently satisfied with what he saw and believing the decorum of his courtroom to have been preserved, he ordered the trial to begin.

Had he come down off the bench to examine the lady lawyer at close range, his victory might have paled. A closer look would have revealed that the scalloped lace was only simulated. Actually it was toilet paper from the ladies' room, cut with a manicure scissors into a fancy design.

At noon, when she lunched with Chown in her private dining room, Mrs. Root startled him by saying, "Jim, get up a party tonight for the baseball game. Box seats. The best."

Chown nearly choked on a piece of fish. His mouth opened to hang slack for a moment while he stared at the woman across the table.

"Baseball?" was all he could say.

Mrs. Root said matter-of-factly, "Certainly," pointing out, "it's an American tradition," and proceeded to discuss the guest list.

To the best of Chown's knowledge, Mrs. Root had no comprehension of current events. Should Paraguay declare war on the United States, she would be the last one to find out. She couldn't have named or identified the most prominent of movie or television stars if she met them face to face. Of

sports she knew nothing, including the rules or the participants. In her home, magazines and newspaper lay unopened,
gathering dust. She simply had no time for anything unrelated to work.

Chown, to please her sudden whim, went to the telephone
and, using the open-sesame name of Gladys Towles Root, he
managed to reserve a dozen choice seats for the contest that
night.

"Who is the underdog?" Mrs. Root inquired.

"Houston must be," Chown speculated. "The team is in
ninth place and the Dodgers are in first."

"Then I'm for Houston," she said quickly.

"Naturally," Chown said.

From the moment she entered the brilliantly lighted
Dodger Stadium at Chavez Ravine, Mrs. Root soaked up the
excitement of the crowd. Her eyes were bright and her head
twisted in all directions.

"Bring me everything fattening," she said to Chown.
"Peanuts, popcorn, hot dogs . . . anything else you can think
of."

The first batter up for Houston crashed the first ball
over the left-field fence for a home run. Mrs. Root's face
saddened.

"Oh, dear," she said despondently, rising in her seat and
buttoning her coat, "they've lost the ball. Isn't that a shame?"

Noticing that no one in her party was standing with her,
she reached down to tap Chown on the shoulder. "Come on,"
she urged, "let's beat the traffic home."

Chown rose and whispered in her ear, "The game is only
starting."

"Starting," she exclaimed, shaking her head, "oh, no,
they've lost the ball and the game's over."

Chown gently forced her down into her seat. "Mr. Walter
O'Malley has hundreds of baseballs," he explained in low
tones. "They're going to continue playing."

Her face lit up like a happy child's. "Good," she said. "I'll have another hot dog, please."

Driving home after the game she suddenly asked, "Who is this Mr. Walter O'Malley?"

The identity of the Dodger owner was explained.

"Isn't it thoughtful of him to have all those extra baseballs around," she remarked.

The morning after the night of baseball saw her in court defending a young man on a burglary and rape charge. The plaintiff—an attractive girl—had fixed the time of the alleged act at one A.M. Serving on the jury were four women, and to Mrs. Root the quartet seemed formidable opposition who might consider all men beasts and feel dedicated to preserving the sanctity of American womanhood.

Following one another to the witness stand, the mother and father of her client told similar stories in effecting an alibi:

"We were awakened by a gnawing sound coming from underneath our son's bedroom door. Opening the door, we saw him asleep."

"What time was it?" Mrs. Root asked.

"About one o'clock in the morning."

"How do you know the time?"

"Because as we turned on the light we looked at the clock."

"What was the cause of the gnawing sound?"

"Rats."

The parents claimed patches of wood had been chewed off the door by the rats. The District Attorney was quick to challenge their alibi.

"Did you see the rats?" he questioned.

"No," came the admission, "but droppings were left behind."

In an attempt to show that the markings were not made by animal teeth, the prosecution had the entire door brought into court. The District Attorney displayed several types of chisels that he contended could imitate these markings.

To counteract the attack on her alibi witnesses, Mrs. Root led a parade of rodent specialists and extermination experts to the stand. Finally, one witness clinched the case for her— a rodent authority who had examined and recommended that a nearby house be condemned because the neighborhood was infested with a particularly destructive species of rats. At Mrs. Root's request he had brought along a caged specimen —one of the same variety that had chewed the door.

The jury shuddered upon viewing the fearsome rodent. In their minds he was capable of tearing loose, chewing, and masticating even the metal hinges of the door.

Her next client-of-the-week was a circus aerialist charged with assault with intent to commit murder, who admitted he had knifed a sideshow barker. The high-wire performer and the barker were rivals for the affections of the same girl, a darkhaired beauty of seventeen.

During the trial Mrs. Root noticed that her client kept rubbing the palm of his hand across the sole of his shoe. Her curiosity getting the better of her, she asked about the gesture. The aerialist promptly pulled off his shoe. Inside was a faded carnation wrapped in tissue paper.

"My mother gave it to me years ago," came the explanation. "I always carry it for good luck when I'm performing on the wire. Now I'm depending on it to carry me through this trial."

Mrs. Root made no attempt to deny that the aerialist had stabbed the barker, but based her defense on an examination of his motivation.

She said, "An adult was trying to seduce an underage girl and in order to prevent this crime my client was forced to stop him with the first weapon he could lay his hands on."

Before the jury retired, Mrs. Root conferred with the

judge, imploring that the verdict be returned before the jurors adjourned for dinner.

The judge asked about the urgency.

"So if my client is freed of the charges he can make it to the circus in time for his evening performance," she informed His Honor.

The judge, who probably cherished boyhood memories of circuses, agreed to the request.

The jury brought in a verdict of not guilty. Mrs. Root drove her client to the circus grounds. She sat in the audience watching his act, and before ascending the ladder toward the high strand of wire, he removed the carnation from his shoe and tossed it to her.

Before the week was finished she defended a six-foot-two, 300-pound Negro woman charged by her husband with assault and battery. At the time of arrest, officers expressed an opinion that she could not physically overpower her husband, a man of medium height and weight. She promptly demonstrated that the charges were not groundless by grabbing the man she had sworn to love, honor and obey and turning him over her knee and administering a paddling.

Mrs. Root, while questioning her client before the case went to court, asked what provoked the attack.

"Infidelity," was the answer.

"Did you catch him at it?"

"Nope. When he asks Information for the phone number of a man named Blair, he says, 'B like in Betty, L like in Leona, A like in Ann, I like in Isabel and R like in Rachel.' "

Mrs. Root was bewildered. "How did this have anything to do with infidelity?"

"Plenty," she said angrily. "Those were all names of girls my husband slept with before we got married."

The jury, upon hearing the case, became highly amused, which resulted in an acquittal for the Amazon. Grinning broadly, she started to hug Mrs. Root out of sheer gratitude, but the lawyer, fearing crushed ribs, backed away.

"I got no money, honey," the woman said, and changing the subject, asked: "Do you like chickens?"

Mrs. Root said she was very fond of them.

"Good. I'll pay you in chickens," she promised.

Two days later a huge basket of cooked ducks was left at Mrs. Root's front door. In it was a note:

"Hope you like these as well as chicken, because this was all I could steal."

That same week Mrs. Root refused a case, a burglar out on bail, who sought her services. Listening patiently to his story, she found the tale full of inconsistencies.

When he finished, she shook her head. "Sorry, but I can't take the case."

The burglar in search of a lawyer had a large package under his arm. He carefully untied it and set a dozen bottles of Chanel No. 5 on the desk.

"You like perfumes?" the man asked.

"I love them," she said rapturously. He had hit upon her weakness.

"Then take these as a down payment."

Before she could say no, the visitor, speaking rapidly, said, "I'll just leave them here," and ran from the office.

Acting on a hunch, Mrs. Root telephoned one of the leading downtown department stores, where she herself often bought perfume, inquiring if by chance any of their merchandise was missing.

"Not by chance," the manager of the cosmetics department returned, "but by theft—a dozen bottles of perfume."

"Send someone to my office," she instructed. "I have them here."

The burglar lost not only his case but his loot as well.

Just as Dr. Rudner had predicted, the morning after the discovery of measles started with a flurry of activity. Although Mrs. Root's courtroom calendar was curtailed, she had twelve appointments at home—all with men. Her secretary called each one to inform him that Mrs. Root had contracted measles but would be willing to see him at his own risk.

Only three took a chance.

Finished with interviews, she began taking incoming telephone calls. They were, in sequence: a prospective client in the Central Jail for murder; a writ of habeas corpus on a lost baby; a molesting case; a husband who wanted his wife committed to a mental institution; five horses that were stolen from a barn the woman owner of which wanted Mrs. Root to go out and search for the animals because the police refused, saying they wouldn't know where to look for horses outside of the race track and they weren't fast enough to catch any that might be running there.

In the meantime, remembering that she was entertaining at a barbecue dinner for sixteen that evening at her home and no one had canceled even though warned of measles, she had her hair coiffeured, nails manicured, fixed her own lunch, took a bath and went to the doctor's. On her way home a fire and explosion in a delicatessen called Benjamin's snarled traffic for fifty-four minutes. There was no idleness as she waited in the midst of the line of stalled cars. On her way to the doctor's she had stopped at the law library to pick up two books and now she put in this time researching a point.

The moment she entered the front door of her house the telephone rang. A woman, believing she was dying, wanted her to come immediately and draw up her will.

"I can't," Mrs. Root said. "I have to make salad dressing, bake a cake, bathe and dress for dinner."

Before the woman could protest, the lawyer said, "Get a pencil and a piece of paper. Be sure there's no printing on the top, perfectly blank on both sides. Write what I tell you."

She began dictation:

"Say 'This is my last Will and Testament.' Do not have it witnessed. Be sure you date it and sign it in your own handwriting. Say that you recognize who your heirs are; name your pleasures in what you wish to leave your heirs. Mention them all. If you don't want to give them anything, then just give them one dollar each. State whether you do or do not have any children; whether you do or do not have any legal husband."

Hanging up, she attended to her culinary duties, and while her bath water was running she began knitting something—as yet not identifiable—for the coming of a grandchild.

It was barbecue time and the guests were grouped at tables around the swimming pool. Mrs. Root wore an eye-stopping pink ensemble that might have fittingly been called the "First Rose of Spring." It was made of a Paris fabric decorated with real and artificial flowers and jeweled butterflies and bees.

The snug, clinging, shimmering dress was of iridescent pink lamé flown across the Atlantic by a friend. Two large pink roses, fourteen and twelve inches in diameter, decorated the bodice. The petals of one of the blossoms fluttered down the front drape, which was caught by a cluster of pearls and sequins. Jeweled butterflies perched on the petals of the roses.

Her turban, twenty-two inches by eighteen inches, was made of the same pink lamé material and also bore the petals of the rose. Three large pink roses similar to those on the bodice surrounded the turban. Flying on the petals of these roses were jeweled butterflies and bees.

Forty-five small, real orchids adorned the dress. Her shoes were of pink satin with pointed toes and very slim four-inch heels. Out of each heel grew roses which formed an outline around the ankle and ended in a beautiful bud in front.

One of the women guests arrived in levis. As her eyes

beheld Mrs. Root's finery she whispered in shocked tones to one of her intimates, "Why, it simply isn't the style to dress up for a barbecue."

"Mrs. Root," her friend said, "pays no heed to styles. She sets her own."

Throughout the day Mrs. Root had been expecting a telegram of great importance—word on the sale of property worth five million dollars which would go into escrow provided the principal who was raising the money could pass a physical examination for a life insurance policy. She had a financial interest in the property, a huge subdivision in the Coachella Valley, not far from Palm Springs. Owing to legal technicalities the deal had been hanging in the balance for more than a year.

It had been questionable as to whether or not the lender had a kidney ailment. The entire deal hinged on the result of a urinalysis. If a laboratory test showed the urine to be cloudy from sugar or albumen, the deal would go down the drain and Mrs. Root and other investors would suffer monumental losses.

Shortly after the main course was served, the awaited telegram was handed to Mrs. Root. Chown, who was seated alongside her, lowered his knife and fork, placed them on the table, pushed his chair back a few inches, his face tense.

The long fingernails of the lawyer knifed open the yellow envelope. Her eyes hurriedly consumed the printed words and then she read them aloud to Chown:

"ALL CLEAR AT PALM SPRINGS. NO TRACE OF CLOUDINESS."

Before Chown could offer his congratulations, a female guest gurgled, "What a promising weather report! I must go down to the desert this weekend."

As coffee was being served in the lanai, Mrs. Root was the target of a question that at once cleared the air of chitchat:

"What's the difference between male and female lawyers?"

"Really now, you ought to know that," she said facetiously to her questioner, a man who had been married five times.

After the laughter subsided, Mrs. Root grew serious. The good news contained in the telegram had brought on a fine mood. She began to pontificate:

"There are few women criminal lawyers who have the physical endurance to cope with the daily requirements—this constant treadmill with a brief case under each arm. It's a grind year in and year out that takes its toll on a woman much faster than on a man. There's a climax every hour on the hour and always a series of daily crises.

"Women marry, bear children, are absorbed by domestic life and social demands. It becomes increasingly difficult for them to concentrate solely on their profession. Should they not marry, and so grow into old maids, there is the danger of a warped, bitter outlook which might pervade their thinking.

"Not so with most men. They can become mono-minded, shutting outside influences from their lives."

She paused a moment to decline the offer of a cigarette before continuing: "The chief critics of women lawyers are the old school . . . old-timers. You can almost read their thoughts of: 'What in the hell is the legal profession coming to?' If one of these gentlemen of archaic ideas entered the arena of the courtroom to tangle with a lady lawyer, he'd soon discover that the distaff side is rightfully entitled to its diplomas. Many a male lawyer, when defeated by a woman, will blame it on that mystic factor they call female intuition. This is his excuse. In plain language he faced too much perception and intelligence, and logical thinking processes. Yes, I think that on any single case, if well rested beforehand, a woman lawyer can hold her own with a man."

There was a guest present whose son was a pre-law student at the University of Southern California, Mrs. Root's alma mater. He asked if she had any advice to give young criminal lawyers.

"Well," she began, slowly warming up to the subject, "they have apparently forgotten in the law schools to teach ethics and humanity versus the money. Today the credo of the junior barrister is money versus humanity. I've had many a promising graduate come into my office seeking a job, claiming he wanted, above all things, experience.

"Then the first question he'll ask me is, 'How much money am I going to make?'

"He should serve an apprenticeship of ten years before he commences to think of financial returns.

"When I started practice some thirty-five years ago, it was ingrained in us that we were an officer of the court; thereby an agent of the public, and therefore in the service of taking care of and assisting human rights. A lawyer isn't a shopkeeper. He doesn't sell merchandise. He should not represent a client unless he can believe implicitly in the client. I have never found ten minutes of liberty or life or death measurable by the almighty dollar. To me, it is far more rewarding to win a case with a cause even where only a negligible or no fee at all is attached."

Asked, does the poor man have the same chance in the courts as the rich defendant? Her answer was, "Decidedly no. Even if the abilities of the opposing counsels should be rated equal, the poorer client is outpointed by investigators. Clever hired investigators can mean the difference between a jail sentence and an acquittal."

Touching on the subject of murders, Mrs. Root had this to say: "Fiction and the movies and television have led many to believe that homicides are the end result of careful plotting, where the killer in a premeditated crime has meticulously gone over, step by step, the act he intends to commit. Most major crimes are thoughtlessly contrived or crimes of passion. A large number are alcoholically inspired. The inebriated have a false courage. The Sherlock Holmes type of criminal is nonexistent."

On the jury system:

"As far as I'm concerned, I'd almost eliminate it. There's little milk of human kindness among the jurors. The system needs education. Too many prejudices, too many fixed and preconceived opinions are in the minds of those sitting in judgment on human lives. A jury needs qualified persons in the box. These are hard to find because their first thoughts are not that it is their duty as an American to serve, but how they can escape by presenting acceptable excuses."

On judges:

"Some are excellent; others are not endowed with the competence to run a peanut stand. Since the population explosion has hit Southern California, increases in the number of judges have been necessary in municipal and superior courts. Some of those selected have been political appointees of the Governor. They do not merit their high position."

Of course the matter of dress was bound to come up. "I like to wear a completely different outfit each day right down to my wrist watch," she said. "Clothes I have worn in courtrooms range from fur-trimmed sheath gowns to a fiesta-like Spanish dress. I imagine I could go on forever not repeating dresses. Of late I have had a complete new wardrobe made up every four months. Sometimes I change my outfit two and three and four times per day.

"Many persons have asked me if I wear these clothes for the psychological effect on juries or opposing attorneys. No. I seek to impress no one but Gladys Towles Root.

"I don't mean that in an egotistical way. If I worried about any impression I might make in the courtroom, I could not devote my full energies to my client. When I'm trying a case, that becomes the sole motivating force in my life. People always wonder what I'll wear tomorrow. I don't really know

myself. If my client shows a preference for a certain color—
that's the color it will predominantly be."

On juvenile courts:

"They classify those under eighteen years of age as children. Ridiculous! Some of these offenders are more vicious
than hardened criminals. They need a more punitive approach . . . stern measures so youthful offenders fear what
may happen to them instead of treating it as a lark when
brought to court.

"There's hardly a policeman living who, when he arrests
a youth, hasn't heard the words, 'I'm a juvenile.' To the
teenager this separates him chronologically from an adult and
implies that no law with teeth is going to clamp down on
him.

"He knows he's going to be treated as a social problem.
Consequently, even before he leaves the courtroom, he may
be planning his next shoplifting, mugging, or car stealing."

The final question thrown at Mrs. Root was: "When you
look back on your life, do you have any regrets?"

She answered quickly, "Only a minor one. About two
years after I opened my law office my mother, who chaper-
oned me on all trips, and I were driving to San Quentin in a
Model T Ford. Between King City and Paso Robles the
stars disappeared and a dark cloud blotted out the moon. The
car lights were weak and it was difficult to see the road.

"Something indistinguishable loomed dead ahead and the
next thing Mother and I knew we heard a thump and a
scratching on the car roof. We stopped, as vegetables and
fruit were falling on all sides of us. Believe it or not, we had
gone right under a horse and wagon.

"We talked with the driver. He and the horse and the
wagon, which we helped him right, were unhurt. We helped
pick up his merchandise, told him how sorry we were, and
parted friends.

"I wouldn't have done that today. I'd have handed him my

business card and said, 'If you wish, you have the right to sue me.' "

It was after two A.M. when the party broke up. Mrs. Root undressed and stood before a full length mirror, searching her body for measle blemishes and found a few of them on her back. Then she slipped into one of her frilly nightgowns. Sleep came the moment her head hit the pillow.

Awakening at three-forty-five, she went downstairs to the kitchen and made a batch of fudge.

Postscript

Three alleged kidnappers, who snatched a rich plum in the person of Frank Sinatra, Jr., from across the California-Nevada state line at Lake Tahoe and transported him by car to Los Angeles, were arrested by the Federal Bureau of Investigation on December 14, 1963.

Young Sinatra, nineteen, who resembles his famous father both physically and vocally, was scheduled to entertain at Harrah's, a nightclub, when he was taken at gunpoint from his room.

The trio facing the severity of the Lindbergh Law were Barry Worthington Keenan and Joseph Clyde Amsler, both twenty-three, and John William Irwin, forty-two, who was not at the scene of the abduction. They collected $240,000 in ransom money, most of which has been recovered.

Because they were on Lake Tahoe's south shore in Nevada, where gambling is legal and the odds against beating the house are public knowledge, both Keenan and Amsler should have been aware of the odds against pulling off a successful kidnapping caper. The FBI has solved 64 out of 67 kidnapping cases over the years. The chances of Amsler and Keenan making a killing at the dice tables were far better.

Gladys Root was retained to defend Irwin, the self-confessed member of the group. She was hired by an industrialist, a former employer of Irwin's. Newspapers began running photos and commenting upon her "spectacular hats and garish attire." Television cameras ground, and commentators scrambled for interviews. They were readily obtainable.

"I am always delighted to speak on the innocence of a client," she stated.

At the initial meeting between Irwin and the woman who would try to save him, the prisoner advanced toward Mrs. Root, exclaiming, "Oh, I'm so glad to see you!"

He appeared nervous and distraught from solitary confinement in a cell that isn't long enough for pacing. Most of the time he had idled away lying on his bed. What bothered him particularly was a deputy sheriff placed on watch outside his cell. Irwin is under surveillance twenty-four hours a day.

At this stage of her investigation, Mrs. Root had only scratched the surface. She told this writer, "I will ferret out the entire truth behind the story of the kidnapping. The case is a puzzling one, with nothing fitting into place. There are many loose ends and illogical actions. We may have a few surprises before it is finished."

The kidnap events unfolded like a fast-paced mystery novel. Young Sinatra and his roommate, John Foss, twenty-six, a trumpeter, were having dinner in their second-floor-room at Harrah's private lodge before appearing with the Tommy Dorsey orchestra in the casino lounge.

A knock sounded on the door.

"Who's there?" Sinatra called.

"Room service," came the reply.

As Sinatra opened the door, two men burst in. One brandished a revolver. Foss was tied up and warned, "Don't move for ten minutes if you want to see the kid again."

It was here they first proved themselves amateurs, by leaving a living witness who could identify them, and doing a poor trussing job on Foss, who was soon able to untie himself.

From the state line, they drove in the snow through a road block with Sinatra allegedly on the car floor. After spiriting the boy back to Southern California, they contacted his father at the Mapes Hotel in Reno, where he had taken up a vigil. From there, the elder Sinatra was led to Carson City and telephoned; then back to Los Angeles where the ransom money was paid and his son released.

Speaking of Irwin, Mrs. Root said, "This man is not a criminal type. His mind is broad and open, and he does not think connivingly. He is inconceivably naive. He believes the Sinatras and his co-defendants are going to do right by him.

"He acts the role of an innocent man," she further related. "He is absolutely insulted to think he's being treated as a criminal. Mr. Irwin played a part in a play created for him and unknown to him and he innocently carried it out. He readily admits he was very foolish and that he was wrong in trying to do a police officer's job, but he had more than a passing fancy for Barry Keenan. At one time he had a romantic interest in Barry's mother and had been on the verge of marrying her. He acted as the boy's adviser over the past few years and believed it was better for him to get into it and see that nothing happened to Frank Sinatra, Jr. Mr. Irwin took $48,000 of the ransom money. He tried to get his hands on all of it. His purpose was to return it to the rightful owner. He proved that when he did so. But he got into it deeper than he thought."

Delving into the background of Irwin, husband of Lupe Minjarez Irwin and the father of two children, Mrs. Root said that he admitted to her that he had once been a runner for bookmakers back East. Realizing the evil of this life, he came West to start fresh, and he began to read, becoming interested in a spiritual education.

"I felt," he told his lawyer, "that I had cleansed my soul and had become a rather nice person. I straightened out, married, had children, worked hard every day in my trade as a painter, and my sense of consciousness of doing a day's work and receiving an honest pay and helping my fellow man gave me a nice feeling. I took an oath unto myself that whenever I saw a boy going any or partly astray I would lean over backwards to help him. I can't believe that the FBI says I withheld any information. They begged me to tell them everything. I thought I did."

While young Sinatra was being forcibly held, Irwin claimed to have had long talks with him and liked him immensely. "He told me of the little money he was making," Irwin recalled, "and that he envied me being a painter and able to support my family. Then the boy added, 'I'll bet the gate receipts wherever I sing will go up now on account of this publicity.'"

What will be Mrs. Root's basic defense of Irwin?

"It's going to be a great deal like my defense of Allan Adron.

We'll just stick to the plain truth. Mr. Irwin's intent was a removal and not a kidnapping."

Seeking a reduction in the $50,000 bail for her client, Mrs. Root, in her remarks before U. S. Judge Thurmond Clarke, assailed the kidnapping issue, casting doubts that it really occurred.

Spokesman for the government U. S. Attorney Tom Sheridan said that although all three men are charged with violating the Federal kidnapping laws, Keenan and Amsler are named as the principals and Irwin is accused of aiding and abetting. He explained, "There is only a technical difference insofar as the actions are concerned, but no legal differentiation in the gravity of the crime."

Mrs. Root stressed that Irwin had not been an actual participant in the kidnapping at Lake Tahoe. "We can well say that Mr. Irwin was acting as one member of the FBI," she asserted. "I am convinced that a leopard never changes its spots, just as I am convinced that my client wanted to protect the victim—if there were a victim—just as he had authorized a call to the FBI and asked them to come and get him, I assure Your Honor that he will be here."

She closed by pleading, "I ask at this time of the year [the Christmas season] to return this man to his family by allowing him bail he can afford."

By reducing bail from $50,000 to $30,000, over objections of the government lawyer, Judge Clarke concurred with Mrs. Root's remarks.

"It is apparent to the court," the magistrate said, "from reading and hearing all accounts of this case, that Mr. Irwin really solved this crime by his actions. He could easily have fled over the Mexican border, so I am convinced he deserves some considerations, and it's the best I can do."

U. S. Attorney Sheridan was quick to dispute Judge Clarke's interpretation of Irwin's role.

"Your Honor, it's the government's contention that Mr. Irwin did not solve this case, but," admitted Sheridan, "he was of assistance." He went on to say, "This case would have been solved eventually by the government."

Of the $240,000 demanded and received by the arrested men in ransom money, Irwin said he spent only $31 of the $48,000 he received. "I bought some toys for my kids and something for my wife, Lupe," he stated, "but I had a check in my pocket, and I honestly intended to cash it and make up the difference I spent."

Irwin was irked at the court hearing, objecting vociferously to the government attorney's description of him as an irresponsible citizen who had deserted from the Navy. Sheridan then amended the statement to, "He went AWOL one time."

"I received an honorable discharge from the Navy," Irwin told newsmen.

The three indicted men were arraigned in Federal court January 6, 1964. Handcuffed together, they were shepherded by five deputy U. S. marshals. U. S. Judge William G. East of Portland handled the proceedings. He was brought here on "general assignment" to lighten the burden of other judges.

Mrs. Root was wearing a huge hat trimmed with silver fox fur and a shocking pink dress. The hat became too heavy for comfort and she placed it on a bench in front of the court railing. It toppled off repeatedly, keeping George A. Forde, one of Joseph Amsler's lawyers, busy picking it up.

Meanwhile, Frank Sinatra and his son continue to sing, and Gladys Towles Root will in turn try to prevent a song: a swan song for John William Irwin.